UoLe
Easy 4 me 2

Other books from UoLearn

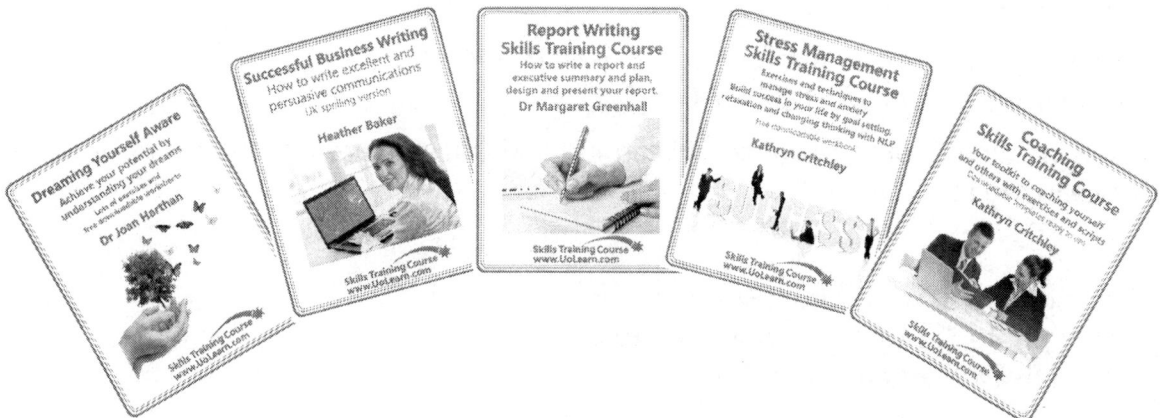

Speed Writing Skills Training Course
For faster note taking and dictation
UK Spelling Edition
Heather Baker
www.UoLearn.com

Developing Your Influencing Skills
A guide to developing the
7 traits of influential people
Lois Burton and
Deborah Dalley
Skills Training Course
www.UoLearn.com

Dreaming Yourself Aware
Achieve your potential by
understanding your dreams
Lots of exercises and
free downloadable worksheets
Dr Joan Harthan
Skills Training Course
www.UoLearn.com

Successful Business Writing
How to write excellent and
persuasive communications
UK spelling version
Heather Baker
Skills Training Course
www.UoLearn.com

Report Writing Skills Training Course
How to write a report and
executive summary and plan,
design and present your report.
Dr Margaret Greenhall
Skills Training Course
www.UoLearn.com

Stress Management Skills Training Course
Exercises and techniques to
manage stress and anxiety
Build success in your life by goal setting,
relaxation and changing thinking with NLP
Free downloadable workbook
Kathryn Critchley
Skills Training Course
www.UoLearn.com

Coaching Skills Training Course
Your toolkit to coaching yourself
and others with exercises and scripts
Download the template easy to use
Kathryn Critchley
Skills Training Course
www.UoLearn.com

Order books from your favourite bookseller or direct from www.uolearn.com

Practical and Effective Performance Management

How excellent leaders manage and improve their staff, employees and teams by evaluation, appraisal and leadership for top performance and career development.
For line managers, team leaders and supervisors to enhance their performance management skills.

Lots of exercises and free downloadable workbook.

Published by: Universe of Learning Ltd, reg number 6485477, Lancashire, UK
www.UoLearn.com, support@UoLearn.com

ISBN 978-1-84937-037-0

Other editions: ebook pdf format 978-1-84937-042-4
US spelling version 978-1-84937-079-0

Skills Training Course, Universe of Learning and UoLearn are trademarks of Universe of Learning Ltd.

Photographs © www.fotolia.com
Cover photo © Lida Salatian, www.fotolia.com
Edited by Dr Margaret Greenhall.

Praise for the Performance Management Course

"It gave me practical tips which I can implement."

"I think the roles and goals section will be extremely helpful to me and the team."

"It gave me the opportunity to focus and take on board information while reflecting on my own practice."

"I am really impressed with the amount of information that is in this book. It feels well researched and has been written by someone who has trained this in the real world."

"Steve's approach is to look holistically at performance management - addressing all aspects of the performance spectrum and linking models and theory with practical examples from his extensive experience of working with organisations. Steve makes performance management accessible and understandable, helping managers to clearly identify how they can get the best out of their people."

"It was useful to look at how to reward staff, what to change to make rewards selective."

"It gave me ideas for taking a proactive approach to performance management rather than only responding to poor performance."

"This should be rolled out to all managers in my organisation."

"Lots of ideas on how to improve performance management in my team- especially using the inquiry approach to action plan."

"Steve gave total commitment and understanding to improve the performance of the college through the people. He was empathetic with staff but always challenging and focused. As his sponsor for the work Steve gave me constructive feedback on how the college contributed to the performance of staff in meeting challenging targets. The college success rates moved from 45% to 80% in a relatively short period of time, a true measure of the impact of performance management."

"I wish I'd had this book 15 years ago. It is so well written and has loads of practical advice for everyday situations. I found it really helped me to reflect on my skills as a manager. Excellent and useful book." Head of IT, Large International company

About the Author:
Steve Walker

Steve Walker is a skilled and experienced trainer, consultant and communicator. In a varied career he has worked in the criminal justice system, in universities, for a small consultancy firm and for the Lord Chancellor's department. Over the last 15 years he has run his own consultancy, providing successful help to a large range of organisations, big and small, across sectors and covering a variety of projects as well as developing other businesses. He is also experienced in one to one coaching with managers.

In his work with organisations and individuals Steve focuses on issues around leadership, strategy, culture, performance, development and teamwork, using a reflective and practical approach that brings the best out of people. He is known for helping managers disentangle knotty leadership issues and dilemmas, using relevant research, experience, fresh ideas and clear analysis and sound communication. In his work Steve's goal is to help people to work out specific actions that they can take back to their real world and apply with confidence, and he has a strong and successful track record in this. He is committed to an effective leadership approach that also focuses on developing people and treating them with respect and integrity.

Steve has covered performance management at a number of levels, from working with senior managers on improving performance across the whole organisation to helping team leaders with everyday front line performance problems and opportunities.

Steve always takes a pragmatic approach to his work on performance management. He makes sure that the advice and help that he gives are useful in the everyday situations that managers find themselves. At the same time he works with people in a considered and thoughtful way, using up to date research to inform advice and actions. Steve is also careful to take into account all of the complications in any issue to make sure that solutions stick: no quick easy wins that lead back to even worse problems.

For some time Steve has been keen to convert this work into a book on performance management that captures his and hundreds of managers' experiences and then goes on to offer real ways to tackle what can be horribly difficult issues. This is a book with a difference, blending tried and tested ideas with rugged, real world pragmatism to help all managers to work on and improve the way that they manage the performance of their staff and their teams.

To contact Steve please email Steve@UoLearn.com

Dedication

I dedicate this book to Josie, Gary and Jean who have been managing my performance for more than 30 years.

Contents

Exercises and action planning

What Works: Practical Research

Notes:

Chapter 1:
Introduction,
"What's the story."

"If you have an apple and I have an apple and we exchange these apples then you and I will still each have one apple. But if you have an idea and I have an idea and we exchange these ideas, then each of us will have two ideas." George Bernard Shaw

Chapter 1: Introduction, "What's the story?"

This book will look at real performance management issues in real organisations, and work on finding realistic and practical ways of tackling them. This is not a 10 easy ways to solve your performance management problems or treble your leadership in a week type of book. Managing performance, helping staff to work better, tackling poor performance, keeping high performers motivated and, bluntly, changing people's behaviours are about the most difficult things a manager has to do. In fact this aspect, managing performance, could well be the toughest part of a manager's job.

I want this book to help you directly in your day to day work. It will build on your current strengths in managing staff as well as getting you to experiment with new ideas. I will introduce pieces of theory and research and help you apply these ideas to your role.

This is not an academic book, it is decidedly pragmatic and practical. It is, though, based on sound theory, practice and experience.

How to use this book

The aim of this book is to be practical and useful. You should work your way through thinking about how the ideas are relevant to your role. Most importantly you should consider how you can put some of the ideas into action and what support you need to do this.

So the best way to take advantage of this book is to engage with the exercises and keep your action plan current.

Exercise and action planning: Connections

Firstly, get a notebook, or open a file on your computer or mobile device and start an action plan. Note down all of the things you are going to try out as a result of the book. Keep going back to these, reflect on how your "experiments" in performance management worked out, what you learnt from them and what options you are going to try next. Also make notes about what your organisation can do to help you as a manager to improve and transform, the way that performance management is done. How are you going to implement and champion these ideas in your workplace?

➢ Then connect the book to your real life experience.

➢ Think hard about how you can change your performance so that your staff can improve their performance.

➢ Be open minded about the ideas presented, collect personal action points and experiment with these.

> ➢ Think about making small as well as big changes to how you manage performance. Look for what sport psychologists call the 1 %ers, the tiny positive changes that we can make that, individually, look pathetic, but if continuously and consistently we do enough of these we can make a significant impact.

> ➢ Think about your further development needs, make a note of these as you go.

> ➢ Think about what support you need to improve the way that you manage the performance of your staff.

> ➢ Make a note of what your organisation can do to help you in your performance management role, and then how you can feed these back to help your organisation to improve performance management and staff performance in a strategic way.

This book is made up of:

> **5 Key Ideas**

Principles, processes and models, these are ways of understanding performance management and a source of ideas for action points, fitting the ideas to your own setting. This is included in chapter 2.

1. Performance management is essential to organisations.

2. How can we define performance management?

3. The role of appraisal and supervision in performance management - delivery systems.

4. Performance management in action - effective habits.

5. A performance management culture in an organisation.

> **4 Steps for Action**

There are 4 steps that need to be followed to put performance management into action. These are looked at in depth in chapter 3 along with their associated levers.

1. Set standards and goals.

2. Measure staff performance.

3. Understand the real causes of each staff member's performance.

4. Take actions to improve performance.

➢ The Levers

The 41 levers are associated with the 4 steps and link the ideas in the book to your own work experience. The trick here is to try to do as many positive things that you can that will progress your management performance. This is sound change management, not just looking at huge changes but also working on the many 1%ers that will slowly move you in the right direction. You will notice that some levers, for example: performance improvement by wandering around and role modelling, appear more than once. This is deliberate and emphasises the impact these can have on the full range of performance management.

➢ Action Planning

These exercises help you to consider and document your options for action - taking the 5 key ideas, 4 steps and the levers and converting them into development experiments for you to try out. Share these with your manager, business partner, mentor, colleagues etc. Review these regularly. Make this personal development a habit- it is how you manage and improve your own performance.

➢ Real Life Issues and Options

At the end of chapter 4 there are some common examples and issues put to me by managers over the years. These are all taken from real life and may throw some light on the problems and opportunities that you face. With each of these I have included some options for action to tackle the issue. You might want to think about how you would respond and add this to my suggestions

➢ What Works

Key research on performance improvement in organisations, that can be applied to your role.

➢ Website

On our website, www.UoLearn.com, you'll find lots of useful resources, including a different approach to goal setting in the coaching section and a free downloadable workbook for performance management that has all the exercises in it. You can also find the summary sheets for the 5 Key Ideas and 4 Steps so that you can print them off and have them beside you as you read this book.

5 Key Ideas

To define and understand what performance management means to you

① ② ③ ④ ⑤

4 Steps for Action

4 systematic steps to take action on performance management

41 Levers

Tools within each step to help you choose what action to take

Notes:

Chapter 2:
Performance Management and Improvement -
Key Principles and Ideas

"Some people dream of success...
while others wake up and work hard at it."

Chapter 2:
Performance Management and Improvement -
Key Principles and Ideas

This chapter will help you to define what performance management is. It will introduce 5 key ideas that form the basis for understanding the core concepts of performance management. These key ideas will be built upon in the rest of the book with the steps for action and levers to help you improve your implementation of performance management.

What's going on?

Thinking generally from your point of view as a manager, what are the key issues around improving performance for staff in your organisation, business or team/department? Just make a note of these. Be real here, not theoretical. What is really bothering you, what are the knotty performance management issues? These issues can be personal to you in your role, or more general organisational issues. Then, as we go through this book, look for good ways of understanding these better and of tackling them.

Exercise and action planning: Issues within your organisation.

Get your action file ready (paper or electronic).

1. List the issues you can identify within your organisation around performance management.

2. For each of them, write two or three sentences about it - think of these as answering- "What's the story" on this issue.

3. Then list all the data you know about the issue- for example, "we are always late on the deadline for this particular product/client" or "in June Gary, my secretary, was transcribing 2 tapes/day rather than his previous usual 3.5 tapes/day" or "Jill has been late seven times this month" etc

4. Then start to work out the key factors or variables involved in these issues for you- for example: "We don't have any policies and processes covering performance management," "We have too many policies and procedures covering performance management," "the type of leadership in my organisation," or even less concrete variables like staff commitment, morale, communication etc.

5. Work out how some of these factors are connected together, for example: "the more we miss deadlines the more morale goes down" or "as the volume of work goes up, the quality goes down" or "the more I give Josie really difficult projects, the better she does, the more work she shifts and the more helpful she gets."

6. Then quickly start to identify some actions you might suggest to tackle these issues. Do not go into detail at this stage.

This exercise should start to give you a general idea of the state of play in your business/organisation around staff performance and performance management. This is a crucial first step.

List an issue: what is the story behind the issue?

....
....
....
....
....

What is the real data behind the issue, be very specific?

....
....
....
....
....

What are the key factors with this issue? Are there any connections?

....
....
....
....
....

Can you identify any actions that could be taken?

....
....
....
....
....

Please feel free either to copy any of the exercise pages of the book or to download the workbook from www.uolearn.com

Key Issues in Improving Performance

There will be a strong connection between the issues and the strategic, big picture context for your organisation. The way your company does performance management can be affected by its history, the problems it faces in its economic, political demographic and technological environment and what it sets out to achieve- its mission, vision, strategic priorities, goals and projects.

This is an important point. Remember, performance management is not free floating. If we simplify a little here; performance management only exists to help the organisation achieve its strategy in the best possible way- to help the organisation survive, thrive and compete. Performance management is not an end in itself. Sometimes, for busy, hard working managers it may seem like it is, "the reason we go through appraisal with staff is to get the appraisal process done and the paperwork finished."

Strong, improving, performance by staff and excellent performance management by all managers are essential to achieving organisational goals. This is not a theoretical point. The talent and performance of the staff is usually the most important resource that any organisation has.

Research has indicated that the great majority of staff want to perform excellently, so when managers manage their staff's performance skillfully they are actually supporting and helping staff to be proud of what they do and to progress their careers. So, although this is a big generalisation, it does seem that most staff really do want to do a good job most of the time, making our leadership in performance management a real opportunity.

What Works 1: Getting it right

Here is a small scale piece of research from a specific area of the Public Sector, from 2002, though the issues it raised may be relevant to your situation. Although it hints at what doesn't work, rather than more positive proposals for getting performance right, it may prompt some thinking and action by you.

In 2002 the Higher Education Staff Development Agency published some research connected to performance management. Many of the findings were based on staff perceptions, but were nevertheless interesting.

See if you can answer the issues raised under each of the key points. Make some notes. Form some options for action to build on any strengths you find from thinking about your situation, as well as around questions you need to answer about your organisation and issues you need to tackle.

Conclusions were:

➢ Performance management is essential for long term organisational success in this sector. However, I suggest that this can be widened to all other sectors as well.

What do you think? What about your organisation, your sector?

....

....

....

➢ However, there was little or no focused or systematic attention paid to performance management- it was not seen as important.

Compare this with your organisation or business, is performance management tackled in a systematic, explicit, well thought out way?

....

....

....

➢ Job descriptions were seen by staff as removed from their day to day reality.

Are the job descriptions for you and your colleagues meaningful? Do they help you focus and improve job performance?

....

....

....

➢ Appraisal does not work, it is a valuable tool in theory but most Institutions have real problems in making it work.

What is appraisal like at your business, is it taken seriously or just seen as an irrelevant chore, a waste of valuable time for all staff?

....

....

....

➢ There was a lack of comprehensive structures to realistically measure staff performance.

How well is each staff member's performance measured at your organisation, is this done within a well understood, clear and helpful structure (eg competencies, number crunching etc)?

....

....

....

➢ There were real difficulties in rewarding high performance.

When a member of staff does really well, above expectations, is this explicitly noted and rewarded in some way? Is there a policy on how to respond to brilliant performance as well as one on dealing with poor performance? As a manager what power do you think you have in this?

....

....

....

➢ Poor performance was not seen to be tackled, it went unnoticed.

In your organisation, is there tight management of deteriorating performance? Is it noticed quickly and effective action taken straight away? Or when staff talk to each other are there usually stories about people who get away with poor performance, lack of effort? Are these stories common? Or is it clear that deficient performance is visible and always tackled?

....

....

....

➢ Good management was down to luck and there was a good deal of idiosyncratic management.

Are managers at your organisation just left to get on with it as best they can, with little or no systematic support? Or is there a well established structure for encouraging and supporting good management? Are there strong development paths for managers in your business? How clear is the definition of good management in your organisation? Is this definition written down?

....

....

....

➢ There was little planned development for managers.

Does your organisation have a joined up development plan for managers, one that is connected to its business context? Does this plan include providing specific, effective and pragmatic development opportunities around performance management?

....

....

....

➤ There was also very little management of managers.

Are the middle managers in your business supported in the way they try to manage the performance of their staff? Are managers evaluated on how well they do performance management, both big picture and with individual staff? Do senior managers see performance management in the whole as an important aspect of the management model for their organisation?

....

....

....

When managers were effective it was seen to be despite their organisation.

Do you, as a manager, think that you are trying to do good, effective performance management against the odds, despite your organisation? Or do you think that your organisation is right behind you in helping you to do excellent performance management?

....

....

....

(Key points taken from Higher Education Staff Development Agency Briefing Paper 96 (2002))

The scope of performance management

What does it connect to?

rewards projects mental-models procedures systems management-support communication people polices performance support development organisational-structure emotional-intelligence culture confidence recruitment ways-of-thinking supervision job-design history leadership capacity top-leadership capabilities strategy training processes technology motivation selection money morale

In other words, pretty much everything in your business.

The 5 Key Ideas

The 5 key ideas are:

1. Performance management is essential to organisations.

2. How can we define performance management?

3. The role of appraisal and supervision in performance management - delivery systems.

4. Performance management in action, effective habits.

5. A performance management culture in an organisation.

These will:

✓ Form a context, the background to our work in organisations, to doing performance management in the real world

✓ Give you some tools to look at how you are now doing in your management role

✓ Help you to see how well your organisation is doing

✓ Prompt you to add to your action plan list, experiments you can try out as well as proposals to push in your organisation.

I base this set of ideas on research and the experiences of many managers.

For each idea you should look at it, think hard about what it means to you and to your business and all the way through identify insights and options for action.

Key Idea 1

Performance management is essential for an organisation's success

Performance ⬅➡ **Response**

Making this connection sensible not stupid

Key Idea 2

How do we define performance management?

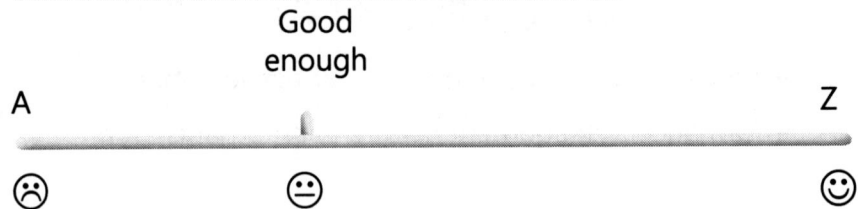

Good enough

A   Z

☹   😐   ☺

Key Idea 3

Performance management delivery system

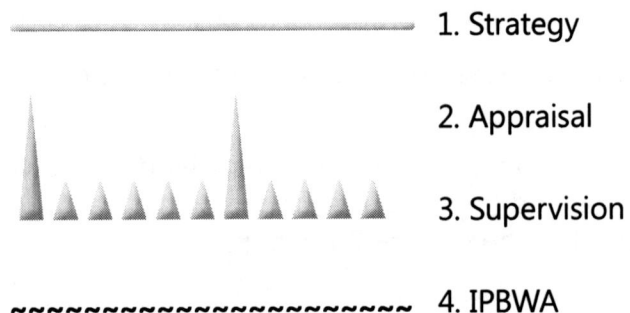

1. Strategy

2. Appraisal

3. Supervision

~~~~~~~~~~~~~~~~~~~~~~ 4. IPBWA

Key Idea 4

Performance management as a habit

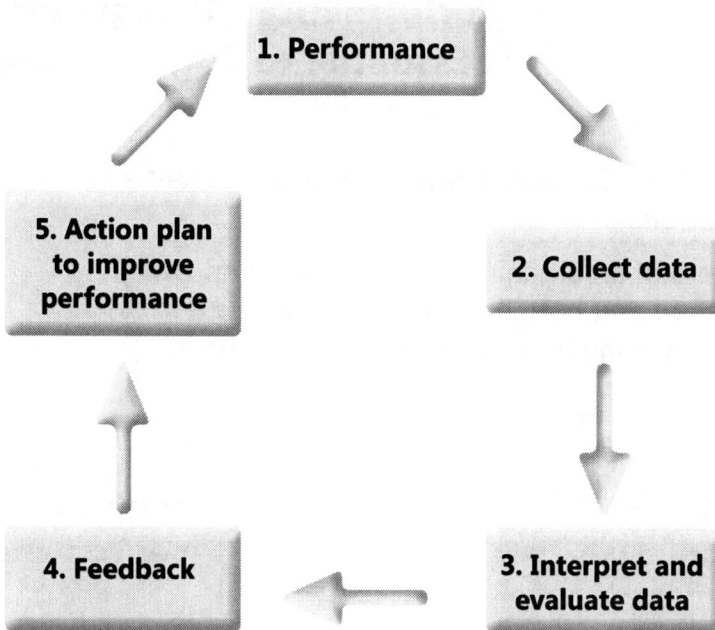

④

1. Performance

2. Collect data

3. Interpret and evaluate data

4. Feedback

5. Action plan to improve performance

Key Idea 5

Impact of culture on performance management and performance

⑤

Key Idea 1:
Performance Management is Essential to Organisations

Key Idea 1: Performance management is essential to organisations

The success of an organisation is linked to improving performance and both are therefore interlinked to how an organisation handles performance management.

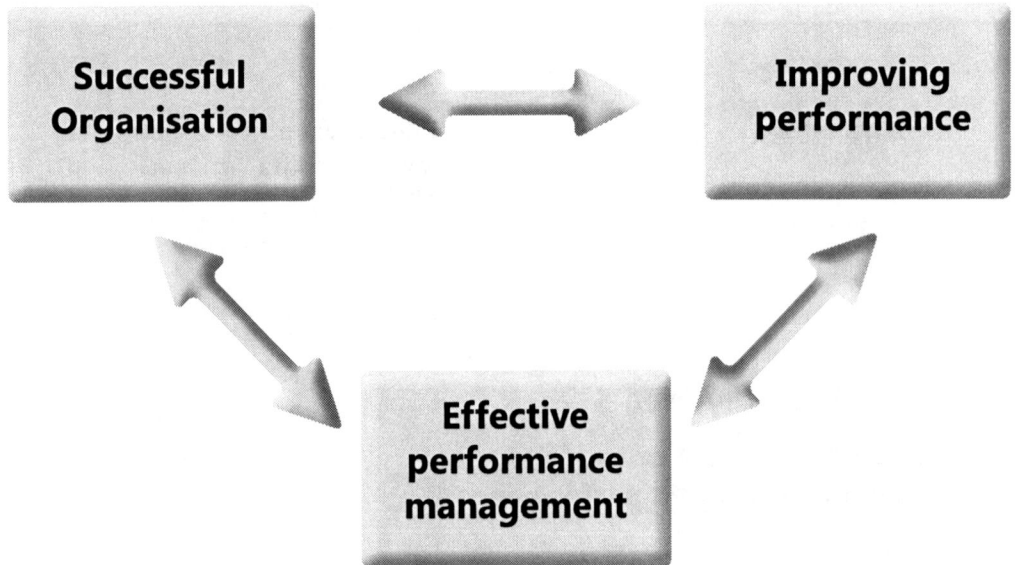

```
Successful           <---->        Improving
Organisation                      performance

                Effective
               performance
               management
```

There is evidence that organisations that take performance management seriously and aim for high standards in everything they do, not only survive but also tend to be successful in the long term.

This is sound common sense. If we constantly look at how the business or the team is doing, keep our finger on the pulse, and we also try to consciously improve corporate and team performance then it seems likely that we will do well even in difficult circumstances. Similarly if, as an individual manager, we monitor how each member of our team is doing and then positively work with them to do this themselves and to keep up performance levels then the team and staff members will do well.

This does not mean that these organisations necessarily have tight, inflexible and hierarchical systems for controlling staff performance. In fact some settings, for example high performing academic and corporate research teams, have been held up as models of good performance management using flexible, consultative and fairly invisible methods.

So it seems clear that getting a strong grip on improving and managing staff performance is essential for any organisation that wants to be successful in the long and short term. This does not mean that getting this right is easy, but it is worth the effort.

①

Exercise and action planning: Priorities in performance management

Either think about these questions yourself, talk to colleagues or discuss with your own manager. Make some brief notes on this, to add to your Action Plan.

What is your view - do you think that focusing closely on each member of your staff's performance and working smart and hard to constantly improve is a key activity for you as a manager?

....

....

What efforts and time do you put into this?
What priority do you put into this area of your management role?

....

....

What priority is put upon performance management at the moment by your business/organisation?

....

....

How could your organisation improve upon this?

....

....

How could you improve upon this?

....

....

Add your thoughts to your Action Plan.

A crucial issue here for you and your organisation to consider is the relationship between performance and response.

| **Performance** | ⟵⟶ | **Response** |

This relationship between performance and response can operate at a number of levels:

➢ Manager to individual staff member

➢ Organisation to individual staff member

This relationship can vary on a scale from

| **Stupid** | ⟶ | **Sensible** |

Options for a response to performance:

1. When a staff member performs excellently they are appropriately and positively rewarded for this. This reward may not simply be money, but could be any number of other things.

2. When a staff member performs excellently there is no response at all- they are ignored.

3. When someone does their job excellently they are punished, for example they are simply given more work to do, more projects.

4. When a staff member consistently performs below what they should achieve they are rewarded for this, for example by giving them less work.

5. When someone consistently underperforms they are simply ignored.

6. When a staff member constantly performs below the level they are expected to there is an appropriate response, the issue is tackled in a variety of ways, from development activities to dismissal.

①

I would say that Options 1 and 6 are sensible, options 2 and 5 are stupid and options 3 and 4 are very stupid.

It looks obvious. What organisation or manager is going to choose Options 2 through to 5? However, these things can happen, particularly in big complex organisations, for all sorts of reasons.

For example, if you are a busy, hard working manager and you know that tackling someone who seems to be performing badly, almost on purpose, who has a reputation for being "difficult" and argumentative, will cost you a lot of time and energy then there can be an understandable reluctance to take action, to just let things carry on. There is little or no short term benefit from tackling the issue. However, in the longer term there will be positive results from grasping this nettle, making the hard decisions.

If we make the relationship between performance and response stupid then we can get anomalous and harmful situations. We can get one staff member working hard and achieving significant, above and beyond the call of duty, goals. Then another member of staff can be incompetent, lazy, uncommitted, for whatever reason. The virus that eats away at an organisation is when these two staff members elicit exactly the same response from the organisation or their manager. It gets worse if the low performer actually gets a better deal.

The costs of taking options 2 through 5 are significant:

➢ Obviously, your team will be operating below full potential and full effectiveness. The team will not be achieving what it should be achieving. In competitive markets, during tough times for businesses, this can be disastrous.

➢ You have no case at all for extra resources. Why should your team get a bigger budget while you are already wasting money?

➢ This failure by a manager can have a significant and harmful impact on morale and, most importantly, team culture. We will see later that culture is powerfully connected to effectiveness, productivity and profit. So, here, we get hit by a dismal double whammy in performance terms.

➢ If you talk to high performers you can get some interesting information about performance management, their organisation and their managers. One point often comes out. High performers want their manager to try to tackle poor performance in others even if this is slow, difficult and not always successful.

Exercise and action planning: Performance and response

Think deeply about how your organisation forms the relationships between performance and response. Go through the options above- which ones strike true? In particular, what specifically is your business good at?

....

....

....

Identify some actions and proposals for your organisation and how you might pursue these.

....

....

....

For your own management, how do you try to ensure that the relationships are sensible?
What do you do well under this heading? If you lapse into stupid relationships, how does this happen?

....

....

....

Identify options for action for you to try out, to build on what you do well now and to address any problematic issues.

....

....

....

Key Idea 2:
How can we define
Performance Management?

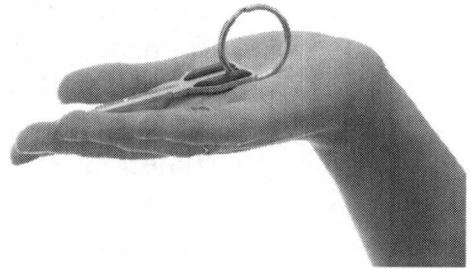

Key Idea 2: How can we define performance management?

We can see staff performance along a line from

A = Very poor, chronically sub-standard performance

to

Z = Excellent performance

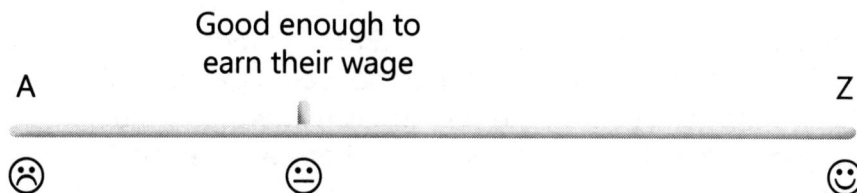

Good enough to
earn their wage

A   Z

☹   😐   ☺

Many organisations think and act as if performance management was just about how poor performing staff are (or are not) dealt with, "What do we do with employees who don't perform?"

Much more positively, managers should think of staff performance management as covering the whole of A to Z. So managers' concern should be with how they deal with excellent performers as well as those staff not doing well.

At the same time the performance management policies that an organisation has should not just cover the A end of the line (for example: sickness, discipline, capability, grievance etc), but should also cover more positive aspects (for example: promotion, staff development and reward).

②

Very often managers spend a lot of their time with poor performers (for good reasons sometimes) and just let the self motivated good performers "get on with it". We can here think about the Pareto Principle- the 20/80 rule. This rough guide says, for instance, that managers will spend 80% of their time on 20% of their staff. If this 20% comprises the staff members closest to A, then they have very little time to spend on the other 80%. Time with a staff member is probably the key asset that any manager has in managing performance.

This approach can have problems.....

What Works 2: Ignoring the Zs

One researcher comments on this, the danger in ignoring the Zs. In the USA Britt found that "employees most engaged in their work reported lowest levels of job satisfaction when their work roles were ambiguous" and they did not get good performance direction and clarity from their managers. "The most engaged and motivated employees were most frustrated by impediments to good performance"

"There is a common misconception that high motivation to work is a personality trait and that motivated people will throw themselves with equal enthusiasm into pretty much any job. Research consistently shows that even the most committed employees will rapidly become demotivated if they cease to find their work meaningful or they can't succeed at it. Managers need to be vigilant about removing obstacles impeding their most engaged employees and actually managing and paying attention to them. These engaged staff were the very people whom they may think need the least help in staying motivated. For these high performers factors they can't control (lack of clarity over what is expected of them, unclear or non-existent goals, inadequate resources) can hinder their best work and may ultimately lead them to seek jobs elsewhere. **The ones who stay behind may well be the ones who just don't care."**

This research may be particularly relevant to high performing staff who have options. It hints that good performance management, paying them attention, is needed to motivate and keep excellent staff. (See Britt for further details).

Key idea 2 implies that managing and improving staff performance is, on paper, straightforward.

Managers need to do four things:

1. **Know where all of their staff are on the A to Z line all of the time.** This means picking up data all the time on each staff member's performance and then making judgements. Remember this is not necessarily knowing where staff are and then being able to prove this in a court of law. More it is using your intelligence, experience and wisdom to make a judgement. Often managers say that because the work their staff does is complex it is impossible to exactly locate staff on the A to Z line. I usually then ask them to really think about each member of their team. Can they place them on the line reasonably accurately, with a degree of confidence? The answer is usually yes.

2. **Continuously move all of their staff from left to right, make sure that they never stand still or move toward A.** This is about preventative performance management plus the development that good managers do with their staff.

3. **Stop staff getting to A.** That way you won't ever have to deal with poor performance. This is preventative performance management again. This is front loading the manager's efforts. Over time this takes up less time and resources than dealing with someone stuck at A, but means a manager has to find the time now to performance manage.

4. **Most of all, never do nothing about poor performance.** Almost always things don't just get better, they get worse and tackling the issue simply gets more and more difficult and other performing team members can get "infected". Many experienced managers will support this view, usually having learnt painful lessons from their early days. Furthermore very often your top performers need you to at least try to tackle poor performance. If you do not their own morale and performance can spiral down and/or they can look for a job somewhere else and we are potentially left with a team of A's!

We will return to these points later. An important rule here in dealing with poor performance is to always consult with your human resources department. We do not cover the legal aspects of performance management in this book and HR people are the experts in this. What they will always say is consult them as soon as possible, do not wait until things have got calamitous.

Exercise and action planning: Reviewing your A-Z

Review your team. Roughly where do you think each member of your team is on the A to Z line? The jobs that staff do are complicated and sophisticated, not clear and simple. So this may be difficult. Nevertheless do try to make a judgement based on your knowledge.

....

....

Are there any to the left of the good enough to earn their wage line?

....

....

How easy or difficult was it to make this judgement? If it was difficult, why? Whether it was easy or difficult what benchmarks/standards/criteria did you use to make your judgement? List these.

....

....

....

....

....

Now add to your Action Plan. What options for action can you think of to improve your management prowess? Be ingenious and creative...

Key Idea 3: The Role of Appraisal and Supervision

Key Idea 3: The role of appraisal and supervision in performance management - "delivery systems".

This key idea describes the essential delivery systems needed for effective performance management. In other words, how do organisations and managers structure and organise themselves to manage their staff's performance. This can be a combination of formal and informal methods. An organisation's systems (for example appraisal) and processes (for example recruitment and selection) should help this delivery system.

Remember these four important points:

1. This idea describes a delivery system. For example, a manager completing their appraisal process is not a goal. It should be a means to achieve the goals of consistently good and improving performance by all staff, with each team member achieving their potential in a supportive culture.

2. This idea is not an argument for lots of formal, bureaucratic rules. I have seen organisations with a plethora of rules, regulations and paperwork around their efforts at performance management. From the outside it can look as if everything is tight and tied down. And yet it does not seem to work, the systems even get in the way of good managers doing good performance management. I have watched organisations that have very informal, understood systems and processes with flimsy flexible paperwork. Yet these organisations and their managers do brilliant performance management and embody this key idea of an excellent, helpful delivery system that helps managers do their job rather than hindering them.

3. The delivery system should be a profit centre and not a cost centre. In other words managers and staff should be confident that although the processes take up time and energy, in the long term they pay back more than was put into them in terms of performance, efficiency, effectiveness, morale, confidence and culture. This is ambitious. However, if your delivery system is a cost centre by this calculation then why do it?

4. Critically, managers need to pay attention to all four following elements, as it is the combination that gets results rather than just using one or two of the methods. Using all components will be massively more effective than just using one, two or even three of them. Please remember this.

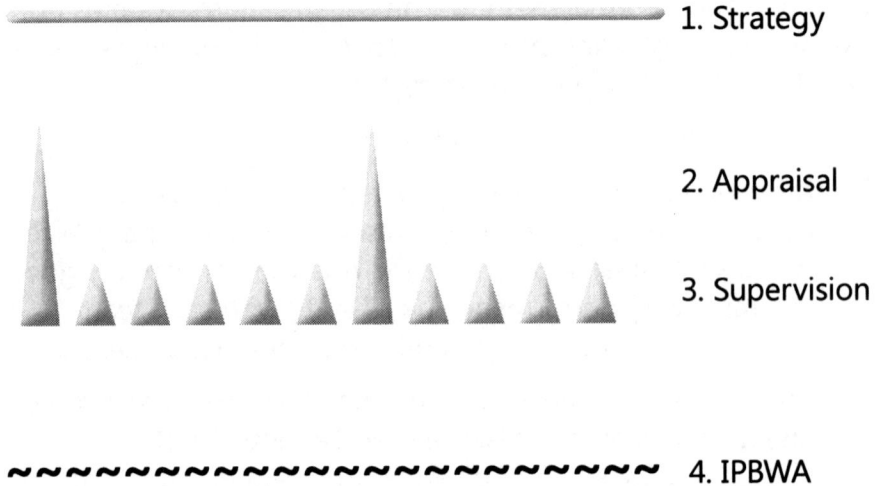

1. Strategy

2. Appraisal

3. Supervision

4. IPBWA

There are four essential components of any organisation's delivery system.

Strategy is an overarching component that helps to make sure everyone is pulling in the same, correct direction, gives staff members important information and up to date news about the big picture and can mean that the conversations that the manager and their staff have during appraisal, supervision and in daily wandering around are high quality, helpful and relevant.

Appraisal provides the goals that you and your team member track during supervision, builds their personal strategy, supports the team's and therefore the company's overall strategy, helps with deep strategic learning, gives focus to a staff member's daily activities as the manager wanders around, and helps make sure that they are doing the right things.

Supervision helps staff to do things right, to make sure that the goals decided during appraisal are progressing, keeps the manager in touch with how and what their staff are doing, keeps the team member in touch with overall team and Company strategy, provides a forum for discussing issues picked up during the wandering around and provides an overall supporting structure for effective performance management.

Improving Performance by Wandering Around (IPBWA) means that both the staff member and manager can pick up issues and useful data that can be used in supervision, appraisal and to inform team and even company strategy.

(3)

1. Strategy: the line

The strategy line across the top of the diagram is there to remind the manager that they should always connect the goals and performance of each staff member with the goals of the team, department and organisation. This means that performance management hits a vital target for you and it provides vertical consistency for the organisation. That is, every member of staff is heading in roughly the same direction, that there is an alignment between every staff member's work/performance goals and the strategic goals of the business. As a manager, working with your team member, you should be able to track a path between the objectives that they are trying to achieve and a specific goal of the organisation itself, even if that track has numerous links in it. This applies to all staff, from senior managers through to first line office support staff, cleaners, receptionists etc. I realise that this can be tricky sometimes as you get to the lower levels of a business. However, in doing this you may also be helping to make a member of staff's work more meaningful, connecting what they do on a daily/weekly basis to what the organisation is in business for. This sounds pretentious but it can work, can actually help staff and contribute significantly to the effectiveness of your performance management.

Exercise and action planning: Strategy and performance

Now go back to your Action Plan. Note ideas to introduce more "strategy" into the way you do performance management with your team. All ideas count, however small. Remember the 1%ers.

....
....
....
....
....

---

2. Appraisal: the tall spikes

This is appraisal. By this we do not just mean your organisation's appraisal scheme, here we are talking about appraisal as an essential management activity. A manager can do appraisal even if their organisation does not have an appraisal scheme. This means that a manager and a member of staff meet to discuss a personal strategy for that team member. Strategy means looking at the big picture for that person.

Typically generic appraisal can have seven key goals-

1. **Accountability**

    Holding the staff member accountable for their personal performance over the last, say, 12 months. This includes reviewing any goals set at the previous appraisal meeting, understanding and learning from both successes and occasions where goals were not achieved. For a staff member this would involve reviewing achievement over key areas of work. For example for a personal assistant supporting a manager, there would be critical, in depth discussion about projects planned at the last meeting and the overall quality of the support given in that role by that person. For managers and supervisors this should cover goals set across key aspects of the leadership role and the overall impact of their team. A key point here is learning from past performance. This would be a non-negotiable goal in any performance management system.

2. **Planning and goals**

    Work planning and goal setting for the next period needs to be done (usually every 12 months, though this can be changed). Under this goal the manager and staff member discuss the essential and optional work goals for the following year. These should firmly connect the work of the individual with the goals of their team/unit/department. Remember this is strategy for a staff member, their key work goals for the next 12 months or so, not the detailed planning of exactly how they are going to do their work. This activity should cover the really important, priority goals that the person should focus on over the next year in order to do

③

their job really well and help their team/unit/department succeed. These could include goals covering the maintenance of current quality standards as well as goals covering new, progressive activities for staff (for example, setting up and running a new project for the business; getting at least three new contracts for the business; improving, by a set amount, the turn around time for a service to an internal customer; improving the efficiency of a cleaning service and measuring this by some good indicators). Research indicates how important this clarity of expectations is for staff in maintaining good work performance and improving on this. This would be a non-negotiable goal for any performance management system.

3. **Professional development for staff members**
   This entails identifying what skills the staff member will need over the next one/two years in order to continue to do their job properly and planning for acquiring them. It is not just an assessment of skill deficits for the staff member. It also concerns the manager looking ahead at possible future changes in the role of staff and therefore, what new skills they will need to tackle these changes. The staff member must develop the new skills that are needed to do their job properly. Additionally they need the support of their manager to help them do this. Therefore, the manager must drive this for each staff member. This goal should be non-negotiable

4. **Career development**
   This goal concerns the manager helping the staff member to set career goals and objectives that they want to achieve that may not be immediately directly connected to their present role. However, the manager should nevertheless pursue career development with their staff, especially as this will help to motivate and retain high performers (see What Works 2). This point is relevant for all staff, at all levels of an organisation. This goal is negotiable for staff; they do not have to develop their career if they do not wish to.

5. **Support for staff**

   Appraisal is an opportunity for managers to provide key elements of support for staff. Not least in providing information to staff that helps them to do their job properly and to improve performance as well as understanding more about the big picture and changes imminent for the business and how this might affect the staff member. This goal is non-negotiable for the manager - whether or not the team member accepts it is up to them.

6. **Joint planning for an individual's performance management**

   The appraisal meeting is an opportunity to plan how the manager and staff member are going to structure their contacts over the next 12 months. The practical details of how often, when and where subsequent meetings will take place will be agreed. In plain terms, how they are going to work together effectively. Taking into account Key Idea 1, remember, managers should give priority to this activity.

7. **Driving team and leadership development**

   Appraisals should give managers the real opportunity to get feedback from their staff about two issues. Firstly to ask staff about their own leadership style, so adding to the manager's self development and improved performance. Secondly to get ideas from staff about team development and improvement. This is negotiable on the staff member's behalf, but desirable and useful for the manager.

As well as all of these objectives, a good performance management delivery system can help in building a decent, fair organisation, a good place to work that treats everyone with respect. Additionally it can also help in maximising how well talent is identified and brought on in an organisation.

> ### What Works 3: Appraisals
>
> An important commentator on diversity issues mentions the role of appraisal. He indicated that: "Appraisal is critical for managing diversity. An effective system can drive up diversity and fairness in the organisation. The appraisal process will determine the language used to describe and evaluate performance" and "will emphasise those behaviours which are considered to be important, those which are unimportant and indeed those which are not valued at all."
>
> So, from this point of view Kandola makes the point in favour of appraisal. However, he warned that appraisals are a one to one process and if not done effectively and carefully, in an organisation without a strong diversity policy, "can offer considerable scope for" unfair bias.
> (see Kandola and Fullerton)

3. The delivery system- supervision: the small spikes

Between the appraisals the delivery system consists of supervision meetings between the manager and staff.

If appraisal is the manager discussing strategy with their staff member, then these meetings are used to discuss tactics, action planning and evaluating progress on the goals set in appraisal.

These meetings can be as frequent as the manager thinks necessary, in consultation with the staff member, remembering that the manager should have the final say in this. Obviously, the meetings will be more frequent for a new, junior member of staff than for an experienced, highly competent one. The frequency, format and venue for these meetings would be decided under Goal 6 for appraisal.

Any organisation's policies should allow for both the above type of meetings with staff, and for the flexibility that is needed to make them work. However, in my experience, some organisations have policies that are so inflexible that they do not allow this, they operate a one size fits all approach that does not work, that does not represent effective performance management.

Exercise and action planning: Goal planning

Think about one or two members of your team. What goals do they have for the next 12 months or so? If you do not know this already, then what goals do you think that they should have? Write these down.

What are the strategic goals of your business for the next one to five years? Write these down.

Now link the answers from part 1 to those from part 2 above as specifically as you can, and write these down.

③

For example, for a fee earning lawyer in a medium sized law firm:

Goal 1 for staff member: "Over the next 12 months will bring in client fees of at least £98,000."

Achievement of this will contribute to her team goal of achieving a turnover of £270,000.

Which in turn will contribute to the firm's Strategic Aims:

1. Making a profit of £X this year and
6. Open new office in neighbouring town by end of year.

Goal 2: "Over the next 12 months they will build an effective team with a positive, supportive, performance based culture."

This will contribute (probably) to all of the team goals

These will obviously contribute to all or most of the firm's goals, for example one that could read: "This firm will be a positive, exciting and rewarding place to work for all staff."

4. IPBWA, Improving Performance by Wandering Around: the curves ~~~~~~~~~~~~~~~~~~~~

This is a version of a well known management model, management by wandering around, something all good managers will do, leaving their offices and paperwork and meetings frequently to talk to and help their staff and keep up to date with what's going on. This can extend to noticing the service that your customers get, gathering data from the front line of your business.

IPBWA means improving performance by wandering around. It is hard to overestimate the impact that this informal method of paying positive attention to staff can have, if done with genuine interest. One large piece of research, focused on highly effective and successful managers indicated that they had a performance management routine. A key aspect of this routine was that it encouraged as many contacts, both formal and informal, with staff as was humanly possible.

With slight differences between different types and levels of staff, these four delivery mechanisms should combine together to form a system that helps managers to do effective performance management and therefore to improve staff performance.

What Works 4: The Hawthorne Effect

In the 1920s, in the USA, researchers looked for ways to improve the performance of a group of women workers in a factory. Their findings were interesting and a little confusing in that:

Nothing that was done seemed to have any real impact on performance.

Except that the fact that the researchers singled them out from the other workers and paid genuine attention to them actually had a positive impact on the performance of staff that were studied.

This has become known as the Hawthorne effect.

For managers it can mean that we might be able to improve our staff's performance through:

➤ Frequent contacts

➤ Paying genuine, real attention, showing an interest.

Furthermore this is cheap in that it does not cost any money. It does, though, cost time. However, the hope here is that in the longer term this cost is paid back through improvements in team and individual performance and by the way it can make for a better team culture, "The way we do things round here."

What Works 5: Delivery system

One researcher, Paul Ramsden, commented on some aspects of this performance management delivery system.

"A good performance management delivery system is concerned with enabling people to learn, helping them transform their understanding, helping them address change and helping them link their own development and performance to the work unit's and their organisation's goals. It should encourage reflection collaboration and problem solving. It should merge the management of the individual with the management of the organisation. It cannot be carried out by a once yearly meeting but must be integrated with the day to day work of the department. Paperwork should be minimal and effective performance management is embedded in a (suitable) organisational culture.

A performance management system that is not owned by staff or believed to be beneficial rather than a time wasting device cannot work."

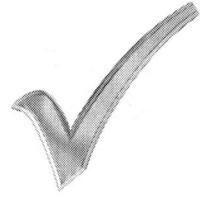

Exercise and action planning: Key Idea 3, The role of appraisal and supervision in performance management-"delivery systems".

Critically review your delivery systems for performance management and for improving the performance of all of your staff. How well do they work?

....
....
....
....
....
....
....
....
....
....

In order to improve the performance of your staff, what do you need to keep doing in terms of this key idea?

....
....
....
....
....
....
....
....
....
....

To improve the performance of each of your staff, again focusing on this key idea, what do you need to stop doing?

In terms of this key idea, what new actions can you take to improve staff performance?

Add these to your action plan, then take them to work and experiment.

**Key Idea 4:
Performance Management in
Action - Effective Habits**

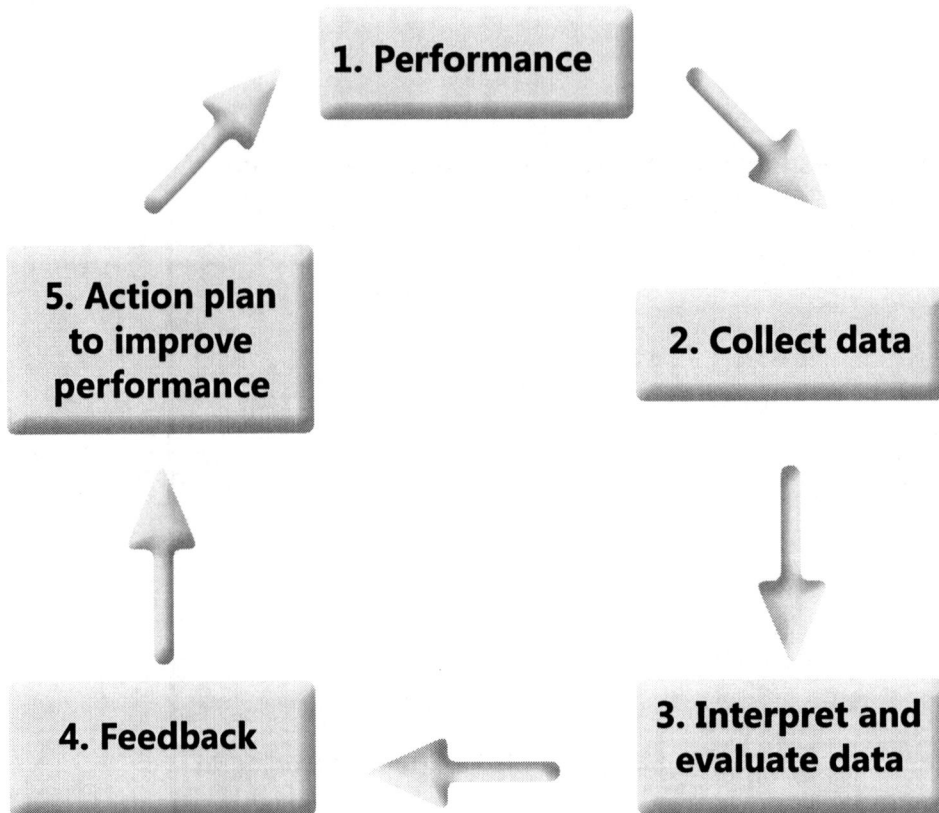

1. Performance

2. Collect data

3. Interpret and
evaluate data

4. Feedback

5. Action plan
to improve
performance

This key idea covers managers focusing on improving their staff's performance as a cyclical habit that they do every day, throughout all of their contacts with staff. It is a version of IPBWA from Key Idea 3. Incorporating performance management as a habit, something you do as a manager pretty much all the time, can lift your effectiveness, improve staff and team performance, contribute to team culture and help you manage your most valuable personal resources, your time and intelligence.

This idea presents a rough structure to help you implement this habit, so that it becomes "unconscious competence", an effective part of your performance management that you do without thinking about it.

The habit means (see the diagram):

1. Staff perform, they make things, sell things, do reception, support other staff, write programs, fix things, clean, deal with customers, do paperwork, do casework with clients, project management, teach, answer the phone, write things, do presentations, run homes for elderly people, practice law with clients, manage staff, manage finances, paint and decorate, sort computer problems etc.

2. Then the manager will collect data. They will observe, read evaluations, get messages from other parts of the organisation etc, reviewing all sources of performance data that they can get. The data can be hard (number crunching) or soft (observations, discussion points). Both these sets of data are equally important. Collecting examples of "soft data" (eg walking through the office and noting a phone ringing and no one bothering to answer it or seeing a new member of staff on reception dealing expertly with a troublesome customer or just noticing how well staff engage with each other in solving everyday problems or how staff respect each other in everyday office life) can give you a good idea of team culture. As we will cover later, culture is an important aspect of both team performance and performance management in itself.

3. Now the manager must start to work out, analyse and understand, judge what the data means about that staff member's performance and, sometimes, about overall team performance. Data is not obvious and neutral, we need to get below the surface, get at real understanding. For example, in the academic world, below average student evaluations of a particular course could mean that the lecturer was under-performing. It could also mean that the course was particularly intellectually challenging and students were reacting to this, rather than the strength of the staff member's teaching performance. Complaints by staff could mean that a cleaner was not performing adequately. However, it could also mean that the staffs' expectations were too high or the cleaner simply had too much work for the time they had available. It is important that this habit is worked sensitively and intelligently by the manager.

4. Working with the staff member, the manager then needs to feedback their judgements. See later in the book for further ideas about giving effective feedback.

5. The outcome of the feedback should be specific actions for the staff member that will help them to repeat good performance or, when relevant, improve performance.

We then get back to Stage 1 of the habit and the cycle begins again and so on and so on .....

Tips for making this habit work:

✓ Make the opportunities to drive this habit round time and time again every day with every member of staff, as part of improving performance by wandering around (see Key Idea 3).

✓ Keep practising going round the steps, for both big and small events that you encounter- make it so the cycle is second nature, an unconscious habit. Remember the 1%ers.

✓ The habit should be focused on examples of both below standard performance and excellent performance. The goals are to improve continuously the performance of each member of your staff and to work on their and your learning and development.

✓ This habit can be a cheap way of performance development and improvement- managers can go round the cycle as part of their everyday work. It can be integrated into the working day. Don't just walk to a meeting in another part of the business, use the journey to start going round the cycle as far as you can get. Remember the 1%ers.

✓ All of the five stages need to be considered in turn, none can be missed. For a manager, there is no point in noticing a staff member dealing poorly with a situation, analysing what happened and why, and then not feeding back or working out a specific action plan to help the staff member change.

✓ Sometimes, because of the pressures of work you may not be able to complete the cycle in one go. Keep a notebook so that you remember to eventually complete the cycle. If you do not have time or opportunity immediately, do phase 1 and 2, go away and think about phase 3 and then arrange a time to do phases 4 and 5 with the team member.

✓ Remember, feedback is rarely useful unless it leads in some way to specific action points that the staff member can actually use.

Exercise and action planning: Performance review

Critically review your own performance as a manager.
How well do you think you drive this habit?
What helps you and what hinders you from doing this?

....
....
....
....
....
....

Review- What are the key points that you want to tackle?

....
....
....
....

What Helps?

....
....
....
....

What Hinders?

....
....
....
....

Do you get good feedback that helps you improve your management performance? Why does this work for you? What actions do you need to take to improve the feedback that you get?

....

....

....

....

Bring this reflection together and add some options to your Action Plan, and then experiment.

....

....

....

....

One idea that some managers use is to consciously apply the habit for, say, the next two weeks at work and then review how it went, what you have learnt from it and how you can put that learning into action in your future performance management.

Think about asking your staff about how well you help them to improve their performance using this Key Idea. There is an important point here- if a manager is not open to receiving feedback and acting on it, then their staff will probably be similarly resistant.

Key Idea 5:
A Performance Management
Culture in an Organisation

The aim here is for you to build a culture or climate in your team that positively helps all staff to continuously improve their individual and collective performance and therefore helps you to do strong, subtle and effective performance management.

The climate or culture in an organisation is the sum of the informal behaviours or habits and the perceptions that staff have in that organisation. It has been called "the way we do things round here". You can sometimes get an idea of the climate by the stories that staff tell about various issues, in this case around performance management. What stories go round your organisation (see the very first exercise)?

Sometimes an organisation will have a corporate climate, a common culture that runs through the whole of the organisation. So, for example, there may be elements of climate that most, if not all, academics share across a university. Indeed this core climate may be shared by academics across a number of institutions- it may be almost a national academic culture. Or there may be a core culture that the sales staff in a business work to. Again this might even be national. Or a culture shared by the lawyers in a firm and, perhaps, a different one shared by the support staff there. As well as this, organisations may have different cultures across different departments as well as categories of staff. The overall climate may be made up of multiple cultures.

Culture is important to performance. One researcher into organisations, Daniel Goleman, alleged from his research that in manufacturing a positive culture could make as much as a 30% improvement in productivity. In other words, there

was a significant performance uplift that did not seem to have anything to do with resources, finances, hardware etc. Goleman's later work strongly implied that the key factor in forming this performance enhancing climate was leadership. In other words, the way that you do leadership in general and, of course, performance management specifically has a real impact on performance, productivity, effectiveness and profit.

One of the ways that this leadership works on performance is the way that you, as a manager and leader, mould the culture in your team. This alone makes this key idea important and useful.

Part of a positive culture is how staff deal with the informal aspects of performance management and performance improvement.

What Works 6: Culture

One organisation I have dealt with, taking on the importance of culture in performance improvement, set out to consciously build a more supportive climate. It's explicit aim was:

"... To build our culture so that it has a strong performance, learning, development and supportive ethos. This culture is focused on quality of service to both clients and each other as well as having a strong innovative and a questioning, curious strand. All staff will continuously and consciously build on this culture with managers taking on an essential role in this."

What might a positive performance culture look like?

It seems clear then that a key part of any manager's role in any organisation is to build a positive culture in their team. An important strand of this culture will be how well it promotes continuously improving performance across all team members. Staff members who consistently work on improving their own performance without the direct push from their manager will usually be a sign of a positive climate.

65

What Works 7: Questions for a culture of improving performance

Paul Ramsden, an academic writing about UK Universities, comments on what an improving performance culture might look like for academics. I include this here because it almost certainly has some general applicability, especially in businesses where staff are moderately autonomous and need to be creative and innovative.

Performance management, what an institutional culture should encourage team members to ask:

Objectives: What goals do I want to achieve this year in my career?

Delegation: What power, resources and authority do I have to make them happen?

Work Plans: What are the best routes to achieving my career goals?

Training: What new skills and knowledge do I need to achieve these things?

Facilitation: What specifically will my manager do to help me achieve my career goals?

Feedback: What specific feedback can I expect from my manager?

Tracking: What is the best way of measuring my progress?

Recognition and rewards: What response and recognition will I get for my accomplishments?

Development: How can I prepare myself to move up to a higher and more difficult role?

Exercise and action planning: Questions for your team

Think about your team. Do they regularly ask these questions of themselves and in conversations with you?

....

....

....

....

Do you encourage, help them to discuss these issues with you?

....

....

....

....

Now move again to your Action Plan- what options can you identify to work on your team performance culture and, specifically, to get staff really involved in the core questions outlined in What Works 7.

What Works 8: Climates in effective organisations

Daniel Goleman, looked at strong climates in effective organisations. His key point was that:

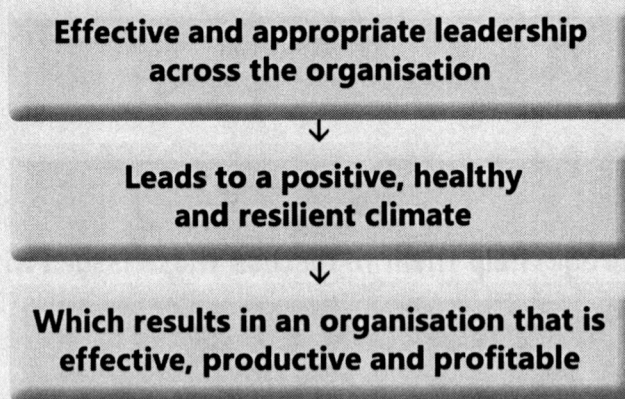

Effective and appropriate leadership across the organisation

↓

Leads to a positive, healthy and resilient climate

↓

Which results in an organisation that is effective, productive and profitable

Managers will focus on what factors drive a strong climate.

This research identified six critical climate dimensions:

1. **Team Commitment:** people are proud to belong to the organisation and the team, they find their work meaningful and useful. They talk about their work with friends in a positive way.

2. **Clarity:** everyone in the organisation knows exactly what is expected of them in their role and the values of the company (for example, use your initiative).

3. **Standards:** goals are audacious and challenging but just about attainable.

4. **Responsibility:** staff are given authority and power to get things done, power is passed downwards in a company.

5. **Flexibility:** there are no unnecessary rules, policies and procedures and initiative is encouraged.

6. **Rewards:** staff are recognised and rewarded for good performance, the relationship here is sensible.

When staff rate these factors high they are indicating that their team is an enjoyable and productive place to work, where they will really be recognised for their performance, they will be motivated and give their best and performance will be high and improving all the time.

Exercise and action planning: Your culture

It could be useful to conduct the following exercise either with your team or other managers.
Otherwise think about the questions yourself.

Identify the key elements of the current culture in your team. Try to use some of the ideas about culture discussed above. Examples could be:

➤ Everyone has high standards and we help each other achieve them.
➤ Poor performance is usually ignored.
➤ We do whatever we can to reward excellent performance.
➤ Top performance only gets you more work.
➤ Quality of service is our most important concern.
➤ It's not worth tackling non-performance, nothing ever happens, you can't do anything about it.
➤ We give each other useful feedback all the time.
➤ Appraisal is really useful.
➤ Staff look out for each other.
➤ We support each other.

(5)

Which of the elements in your team culture support performance improvement?

....

....

....

....

Which elements work against performance improvement?

....

....

....

....

As a manager, what actions will you take to improve your team's climate, and therefore performance?
Add these to your action plan.

....

....

....

....

What could your organisation do to help you change your team climate? Add these to your action planning, including how you are going to approach them in your business.

....

....

....

....

Chapter 3:
Improving Staff Performance-
The 4 Step Model

"The vision must be followed by the venture.
It is not enough to stare up the steps -
we must step up the stairs." Vance Havner

Chapter 3: Improving Staff Performance - The 4 Step Model

In this chapter we will use the Key Ideas to look at ways to tackle staff performance improvement in your team.

I will use a practical 4 step model. For each step I will, as before, present some useful pieces of research. Most importantly though I will suggest levers or options for action that managers can consider and then use, where relevant, to help their staff to improve performance and to tackle poor performance. As we go through, pick out the levers that you can experiment with and add them to your action plan.

Experience and research indicates that to change performance it is more effective for managers to focus on a number of these levers, rather than simply trying one thing. So, for example, just sending a member of staff on a training course, without other actions (such as one to one contact with their manager, support from the manager and other staff, re-examining the person's workload, re-assessing the IT and hardware the person has available, the manager reviewing the effectiveness of their own leadership styles etc) will probably only have a limited effect.

When faced with a staff performance issue, managers have to look beyond the symptoms and the quick fixes and focus on the deeper causes and long term solutions. Good managers look at the whole picture before they try to improve staff performance. Many staff performance issues are complicated. Nevertheless, by being thoughtful and mature, we can deal with this complexity and difficulty and take clear actions that tackle the issues.

Before we work through the 4 Step Model, there are some 'ground rules' that seem to apply to managing and improving performance.

Rough ground rules for performance management

1. To improve performance always press a number of levers, not just one.

2. Never do nothing. This applies to improving poor performance as well as managing excellent performers.

3. There are no right answers, no one magic formula. Managing performance is about the manager's judgement in choosing which levers to pull and how hard.

4. Staff are different and may need a different choice of levers.

5. Today's real performance problems come from yesterday's superficial, easy quick fixes.

6. The easiest way out usually leads back to the problem. Good performance management is most often about managers making the hard decisions and choices.

7. Cause and effect of performance issues are sometimes not closely related in time and space. To understand the issues properly (and so then press the right levers) managers need to think as well as act.

8. Which leads to, always think hard before acting on performance issues. Real inquiry (see Lever 4.16) is relevant here- describe, analyse and understand before making judgements and then taking action. If we don't do ground rule 8, we can easily make things very much worse.

9. The best levers are often the least obvious ones- think and act creatively. This can be especially true in motivating high achievers to continue to perform excellently.

10. Always look at the whole picture about staff performance, all of the possible variables, or you will not understand properly what is going on and therefore you may not press the right levers or enough of them.

11. When tackling performance issues, particularly long standing, deep ones, it is useful to remember that "Things will usually get worse before they get better," an old cliché that is nevertheless very often true.

12. Finally, the mark of an effective manager is how willing they are to make hard decisions, take difficult options, rather than the apparently easy route. This is particularly true for managing performance improvement.

Exercise and action planning: Applying the ground rules

The ground rules are meant to be rugged pointers that can help us to manage performance effectively.

Looking at the ground rules, how do they relate to the way you manage performance?

Are there any actions to add to your management role?

The 4 step model

Step 1:

Set standards and goals

↓

Step 2:

Measure staff performance

↓

Step 3:

Understand the real causes of each staff member's performance

↓

Step 4:

Take actions to improve performance

Step 1:
Set standards and goals

Levers in step 1:

1.1 Goals and roles- getting clarity and purpose into performance.

1.2 Strategy- getting alignment between a team member's work performance and the goals of the organisation.

1.3 IPBWA- Improving performance by wandering around.

1.4 Recruitment and selection- the crucial first stage in performance management, preventing difficult issues happening.

1.5 Using induction to prompt good performance.

1.6 Using external standards.

1.7 Culture's role in performance.

1.8 Role modelling excellent performance.

1.9 Diversity issues and performance management.

1.10 Using the rule of 3.

For each Lever you should:
✓ Review its relevance to you in the real world.
✓ Decide if you are going to use it in your real life management practice. Try to be open minded here- look for experiments in using these levers.
✓ Identify and document some options for action for the lever and add them to your action plan.
✓ Decide how you will evaluate your own performance in improving staff performance in using the lever. Where can you get feedback from? Add this to your action plan.

The first step for managers in improving the performance of their staff is to:

> ✓ Set clear standards that differentiate between acceptable and unacceptable performance and behaviour across the whole of a staff member's role.
>
> ✓ More positively, by setting progress goals for staff, achievements above good enough standards.

Most ideas and research about effective management point firmly to a very strong focus on goals and outcomes. Further it also seems that most staff find having clear, achievable and challenging goals, which their manager helps them set and then supports them to attain, very motivating. This seems to apply to all types and levels of staff.

It is hard to overestimate how effective goal setting can be in progressively improving staff performance. This works particularly well for high achievers, for staff close to Z (see Key Idea 1). For staff close to A, setting really clear standards around what the organisation will and will not accept is not only useful in improving performance but is essential if some form of disciplinary or capability action might result in the long term. Setting clear standards for all staff behaviour is also clearly important for equal opportunities and diversity issues. So, for example, your organisation's diversity and equality policies will require managers to be clear with all staff about what is wanted from them and to play fair across staff, regardless of who they are. Ambiguity of expectations can lead to unfair different treatment of staff.

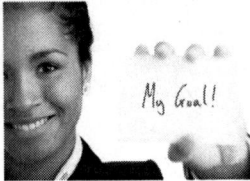

Lever 1.1: Goals and Roles

This technique can be used with staff at appraisal (see Key Idea 3) and will provide them with:

✓ A set of work goals for the next one to two years, a work programme for that member of staff.

✓ Some key development and career goals for the member of staff.

✓ How their role connects with team/department/ organisational strategy as well as the work programmes of their colleagues.

✓ Generally, a very high degree of role clarity.

To use this technique, a manager needs to work through four stages with each member of staff.

Stage 1: Job purpose

Stage 2: Key roles

Stage 3: Manager and staff member begin to set goals

Stage 4: The manager and staff member now review their role map goals and roles

Stage 1: Job Purpose

With the staff member, discuss and identify their role purpose:

"WHY does their job exist?"

This should not be a list of tasks, but should be a clear statement of role purpose, usually just 2 to 3 sentences.

Getting to this, the manager will need to have quality conversations about the purpose of the individual's role in the context of their organisation. This will have positive side benefits. The fact that the manager is showing genuine interest in their team member can stoke up the "Hawthorne Effect" (see What Works 4 in Key Idea 3) and so potentially push up performance.

Examples of possible role purposes:

Teacher, role purpose: To provide excellent, effective and successful teaching and learning to students and to contribute to their department achieving its strategic goals.

The head of department could have a useful, quality discussion with a teacher around what excellent, effective, successful and contribute mean in this context. This would be a very effective use of both the manager's and staff member's time. It is giving clear direction and clarifying roles.

Cleaner, role purpose: To provide a high quality cleaning service to the business, to do this in a flexible way, and to help the business achieve its goals.

Generic Head of Department, role purpose:
To provide excellent leadership to the department, to improve continuously the work of the department and lead innovation, to keep within budget and to actively contribute to the organisation achieving its strategic priorities.

> **Generic Support Unit Staff member, role purpose:**
> To provide an excellent, effective and efficient service to all of my customers at the business, to help to continuously develop the services I provide and to contribute to the unit achieving its strategic priorities.

> **Generic Head of Support Unit, role purpose:**
> To lead the unit so that it provides an effective, efficient and economic service to all of its internal customers and progresses innovation and change in the Unit as well as contributing to the business achieving its strategic priorities.

Exercise and action planning: Your purpose

Why does your job exist?
What is your purpose within your business?
Write down just 3 very broad sentences that encompass what your role achieves for the business.

Stage 2: Key Roles

Based on the role purpose, the manager and staff member break down the latter's job into key roles or chunks. These are the small number of key areas that the staff member needs to focus on in order to achieve their purpose. They are not individual tasks, they are common sense collections of tasks and responsibilities. We need to think deeply about the role, make more sense of it and then reduce it to manageable key areas. There should be no more than 10.

One of the aims here is to produce structure and some control over complicated, wide ranging and sometimes diverse jobs. Once we get this measure of control, we can then try to focus better on the goals that the team member needs to achieve in order to perform excellently.

We can use this idea to help drive up and maintain high performance by a team member by working on:

➢ **Focus**
Make sure the team member is trying to achieve the right goals, goals that merit attention and fit with their job purpose. Ensure that you have team goals that contribute demonstrably to your organisation's strategy.

➢ **Control**
This can work in two ways. Firstly it gives a manager a grip on what their team member is trying to achieve and can help them to coordinate activities across the whole team, looking for areas of cooperation and mutual support. Secondly, the staff member can also get more control of their own work life, potentially setting up a control/confidence/competence/performance virtuous circle.

➢ **Clarity**
Everyone knows what the scope of the team member's role is, what they are in business for and are aware of the key areas of activity that should concern them.

For relatively straightforward roles, you may want to miss out this stage and go straight to stage 3.

As with stage 1, the process can be important and helpful here. High quality, collaborative discussions between the manager and a staff member here can be as important and useful as the output in building confidence and support in the team. Taking a genuine interest in a member of staff can, in itself, help their performance.

Some examples:

Role purpose

> **Cleaner:** To provide a high quality cleaning service to the business, to do this in a flexible way, and to help the business achieve its goals.

↓ ↓ ↓ ↓

Key roles

| **1.** Day to day cleaning work | **2.** Contact with staff and customers | **3.** Make improvements to role | **4.** Self and career development |

Role purpose

> **Lecturer:** To provide excellent, effective, teaching and learning to students, to progress successful and useful research and to contribute to the Department achieving its strategic priorities.

↓ ↓ ↓ ↓

Key roles

| **1.** Teaching and learning activities | **2.** Research and obtaining funding | **3.** Admin-istration | **4.** Self and career development |

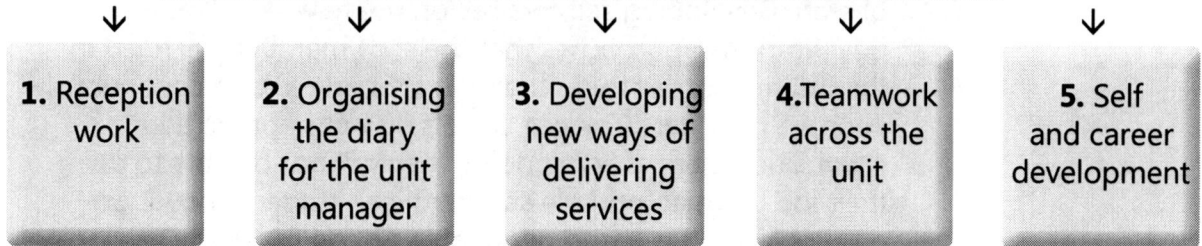

Generic Support Unit Staff member:
To provide an excellent, effective and efficient service to all of my customers at the business, to help to continuously develop the services I provide and to contribute to the unit achieving its strategic priorities.

Role purpose

| **1.** Reception work | **2.** Organising the diary for the unit manager | **3.** Developing new ways of delivering services | **4.** Teamwork across the unit | **5.** Self and career development |

Key roles

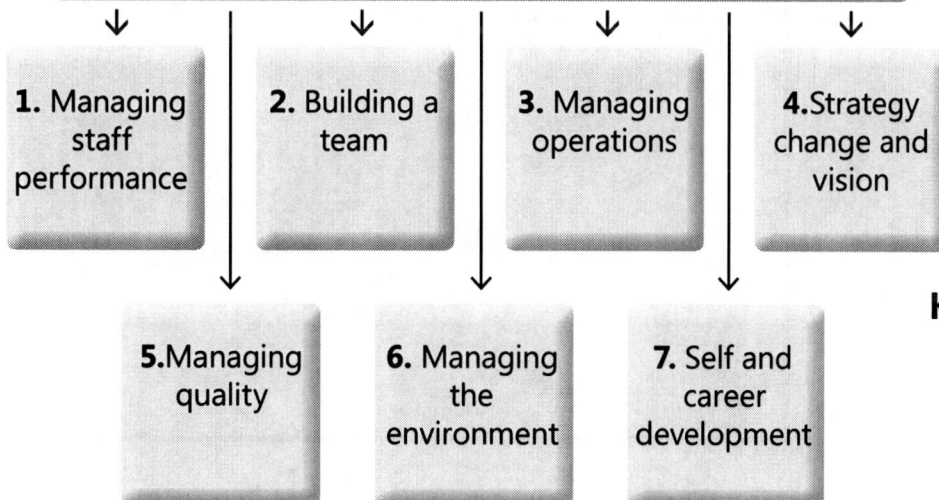

Generic Head of Support Unit:
To lead the unit so that it provides an effective, efficient and economic service to all of its internal customers and progresses innovation and change in the Unit as well as contributing to the business achieving its strategic priorities.

Role purpose

| **1.** Managing staff performance | **2.** Building a team | **3.** Managing operations | **4.** Strategy change and vision |

| **5.** Managing quality | **6.** Managing the environment | **7.** Self and career development |

Key roles

83

The key roles may be different across staff with the same job title, they depend on the exact job of that team member. It is the work of the manager and staff member to customise and complete maps, like the ones on the previous pages.

All of the maps in the examples have a key role covering developing self and career. This is essential for every member of staff. Developing self focuses on the new skills/knowledge/qualifications/approaches that the staff member will need in the future in order to do their job properly and to continuously improve their performance. If staff do not improve their capabilities then, at some point, they will not be able to do their job to an acceptable standard (see stage 1 above). So developing self is a non-negotiable option for staff. Developing career gives a staff member the opportunity to move forward in their own career. Some staff may not want this, so this will be a negotiable part of this key role. However, the manager should always try to encourage this. This key role can be an important motivator for staff.

Exercise and action planning: Your key roles

Based on your own job purpose (see the last exercise), what are your key roles?

Stage 3: Manager and staff member begin to set goals for each of the key roles.

> ➤ Some of these goals will be non-negotiable. The manager knows what their unit/team/department has to achieve that year, and so should have worked out what each staff member needs to achieve in order to contribute to this. So, for example, a sales team manager will know the financial targets for their team and will therefore have to insist on personalised individual financial goals for each member of staff. This is part of the hard decisions of performance management (see Ground rule 12).

> ➤ However, other goals will be negotiable, a matter of give and take between manager and member of staff. Indeed good managers will try to give staff as much space as possible for them to use discretion, initiative and play to their strengths and interests. This will be particularly true when managing talented, high performing people.

> ➤ Some of the goals that appear on the map will be maintenance goals. These need to be achieved by staff in order to maintain standards, to continue good practice. They will not drive the person forward, or change the way they do their job, but are still essential. They are the daily business for the team and its members.

An example would be for an academic:
"Building on my work this academic year on this course, between now and 30th June next year I will deliver History 101 to 100 students and continue to get 95% attendance, average 90% on the student satisfaction ratings and students will score 70% average on continual assessment and average 60% on the end of year exam."

For a cleaner an example would be:
"Between now and 31st December this year I will continue to work efficiently, covering all my work in the required 3 hours, achieving the quality levels set out in the service level agreement."

Goals can also represent real movement, progress for the staff member. These are the goals that really drive change. You and your staff member can jointly ask and then answer-

"What are the really important goals that I could achieve this year that would mean a real, lasting change and improvement to my performance in this role?"

Examples of these progress goals could be:

For a team manager:
"By 30th May next year I will have designed, marketed, implemented and evaluated a new service for the team to provide, and this will have attracted at least 10 paying customers"

For a generic support staff member:
"By 30th November next year I will have redesigned and implemented a new system for improving the quality (measured by asking customers to fill in a short evaluation form) and quantity (measured through collecting statistics) of the service that I give to callers to the reception desk at the unit, supported by relevant and effective information handouts for callers to take away."

For a support staff manager:
"By 1st October next year I will have re-engineered our process for turning around requests for help, improving it from 12 to 7 working hours.

In working on performance improvements managers should try, with their staff, to focus strongly on progress goals, as these can represent real progress for both individual staff, their units and, eventually, the company.

We should try to make goals as **SMART** as we can.
This stands for:

➢ Specific

➢ Measurable

➢ Achievable and Challenging

➢ Relevant to the overall goals of the team/unit/department/
company

➢ Timed

Effective goal setting and then chasing them in a determined
way can help with:

➢ **Focus:**
Everyone is clear about what they need to achieve, and so can
put their efforts in the right place and not get distracted by the
'guff', see What Works 9, on the following page, that usually tries
to divert us. SMART goals can significantly help staff to get this
focus and therefore give them a better chance of achieving their
objectives.

➢ **Control:**
Workload management is less difficult if we have an open view
of exactly what we need to achieve, what quality, how much
quantity, by when and with what resources.

➢ **Sense of Urgency:**
Clear goals with challenging but achievable delivery dates
and deadlines can contribute effectively to moving projects
forward, keeping work progressing. One writer, John Kotter, has
commented on why many change efforts in organisations fail.
One of the eight key reasons that he identified was that team
members do not have, or lose this sense of urgency and sheer
persistence. Work then drifts, and performance goes down.

➢ **Clarity:**
SMART goals can increase staff accountability, if the manager
and the team member know exactly what needs to be achieved,
and to what quantity, quality and timing, then a manager can
track progress, deal with non-achievement, and reward when
goals are achieved.

What Works 9: Barriers to achievement

Robert Pirsig, in his book "Zen and the Art of Motorcycle Maintenance" refers to 'Guff' as the things that always seem to try to stop us achieving the things we think are important. It clutters our lives so that focus can become difficult and we can end up doing the least important things.

Although Pirsig was talking philosophically about life, we can apply some of his ideas to staff performance and performance management. For example, when we hit barriers on the way to goal achievement/performance he says these fall into two main camps:

Set Backs: real objective road blocks to performance. For example the organisation runs out of supplies that a staff member needs to get their work done or heavy snow prevents a team member from getting somewhere they need to be.

Hang Ups: these are problems that the team members themselves "produce". They are subjective, rather than objective. For example, a deadline is missed, performance dips because that particular team member was impatient, careless, lost their temper, lacked relevant skills or failed to plan properly.

These ideas can help a manager to understand what is actually going on when one of their team fails to perform. Was it that person's hang up that impacted negatively or was it a genuine set back? The answer to this can guide the manager's response. Sometimes a team member can try to blame failure on set backs, it was someone else's fault, when actually it was their own hang up. They did not deal with a task carefully enough, they lacked persistence or they did not have a real sense of urgency.

At the end of this stage the staff member has a map of their role, indicating role purpose, key roles and then, for each of the key roles, some SMART key goals. This map will help the staff member understand and agree the really important parts of their job and to focus on the goals that they need to achieve over the next one to two years. This map will then help a manager to manage performance effectively.

Staff Member Role Map

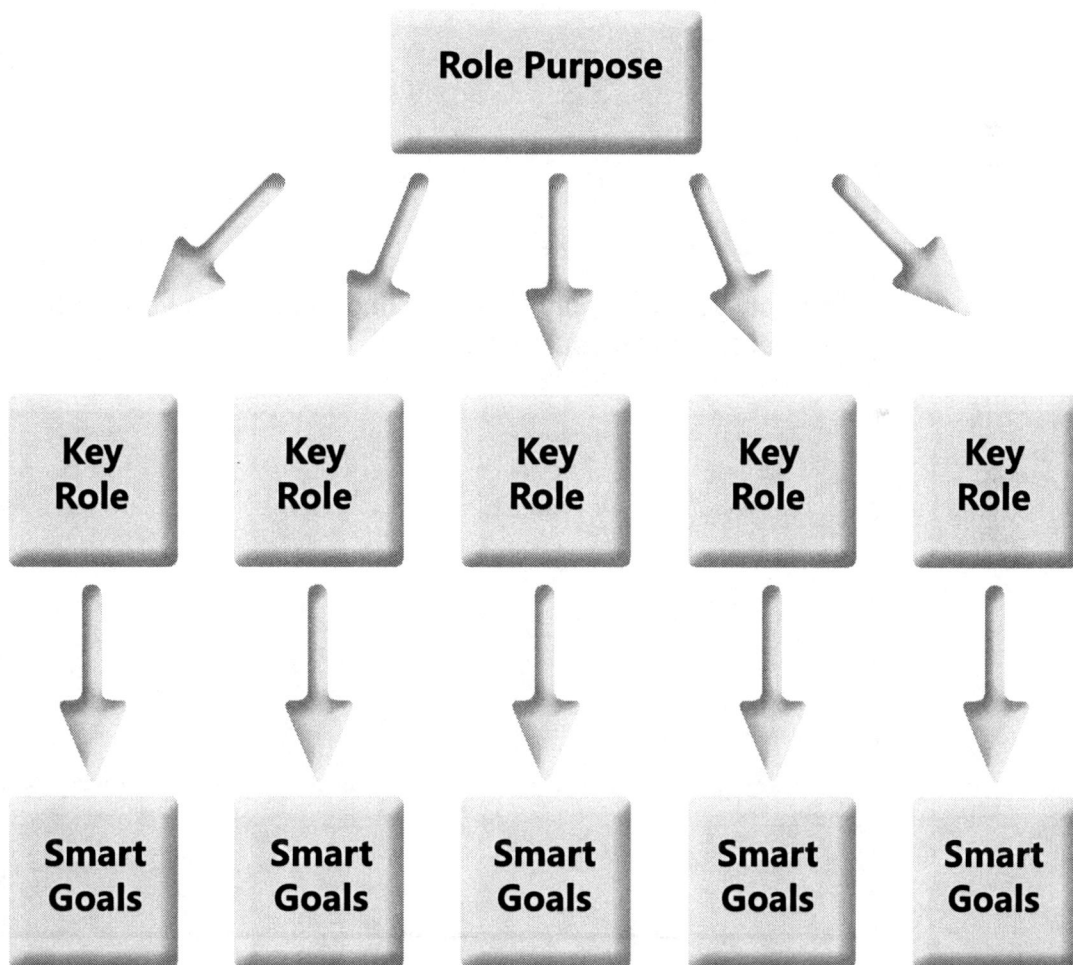

```
                        Role Purpose

    Key        Key        Key        Key        Key
    Role       Role       Role       Role       Role

    Smart      Smart      Smart      Smart      Smart
    Goals      Goals      Goals      Goals      Goals
```

Exercise and action planning: Your roles and main goals

Building on the last two exercises, for each of your key roles list the main goals you need to achieve?

....

....

....

....

....

....

....

....

....

....

....

Plan how you will apply this idea and process to your team members. Add to your action plan.

....

....

....

....

....

....

....

....

....

....

....

Stage 4: The manager and staff member now review their goals and roles map.

We need to make a judgement here. Although all of the goals are SMART, is the overall collection of goals for your staff member achievable? If the role map and associated work programme are not achievable within the time frame then the manager is setting the staff member up to fail. Even previously high achieving staff, faced with this, can be demotivated, cynical and, perhaps, move on. Staff are more likely to over achieve if they are set an achievable programme, and more likely to under achieve or fail if faced with an impossible programme.

If the review of the role map reveals an over optimistic set of goals then the manager and staff member need to radically prioritise, decide which are the really important goals, and which ones can we possible postpone or even abandon. This is the manager making hard decisions (see ground rule 7) with and for their staff.

What is important here are the outputs, outcomes and flexibility.

➢ **Output**

The output is a documented goals and roles map that the manager and staff member can use time and time again during their contacts, it forms the latter's work programme, to be supplemented by action plans to achieve the goals. This can also be used helpfully in the appraisal and supervision processes.

➢ **Outcome**

The outcome is clearly that the staff member improves performance, achieves goals that contribute to team/ department/unit success and drives their own development and career.

➢ **Flexibility**

This model should be flexible. We can change the goals. Some will be ticked off as we achieve them. Some can, because of changing events at your business, become irrelevant, and we then abandon them. In response to opportunities and change we may also add new, prioritised goals.

What Works 10: Management by objectives

Management by objectives (MBO) has been a popular method of raising and managing performance across a range of organisations and sectors. This model can:

✓ Help clarity for staff, it will tell them what they must achieve to be effective.

✓ Link individual, team and organisational goals together in a practical way.

✓ Ensure that staff get feedback on their progress towards goal achievement.

✓ Strengthen the professional relationship between a manager and their staff.

✓ Give some power to members of staff, they have some say in what they need to achieve

The goals and roles model is a version of this.

What Works 11: Connecting purpose and goals

One successful example of an MBO initiative was described by Terpsra et al in an American organisation.

The key points were:

➢ The business was failing, had overall poor organisational performance.

➢ The new top person then decided change was needed to improve performance.

➢ The starting point was to form a practical but inspirational mission for the organisation, an overall statement of purpose.

➢ Then this was taken for each department/team to use to form their own connected statement of purpose and specific goals, covering each of their key areas (covering both front line customer facing and support functions).

➢ Eventually this was then cascaded down, so that every member of staff had their own goals that supported those of their department/team.

This corporate performance initiative seemed to improve the performance of most staff as well as across teams and the whole organisation.

Remember the first section, on role clarity and goal setting was Lever 1.1, ideas you can use to get a better, more systematic and systemic grip on your team members' performance, to help them to improve and achieve.

We now cover some more levers that we can try out. Also remember the more levers we pull, the more chance we have of having a positive impact on our staff's work performance.

Exercise and action planning: Using roles and goals

Look at your own role and goals from the previous exercises. Is the collection of goals that you have set achievable in the time frame for your map?

....

....

....

....

....

How can you use this last stage of role and goals with your team members?

....

....

....

....

....

Add some notes to your action plan

Lever 1.2: Strategy, the Big Picture

Goals and standards for staff should always be explicitly and firmly connected to the team/department's overall strategic priorities. There could be documented cross-referencing of goals. For example, for each of a staff member's key goals (see Lever 1.1) there could be an explicit written note of which team/department goals this contributes to. We can use or amend our organisation's appraisal paperwork to cement this.

A simple example:

➢ **Staff member's goals**

1. Over this year Josie will win five new clients for the firm, whilst maintaining her current clients.

➢ **Which of the Department's six Strategic Goals does this contribute to?**

1. Department X will increase its client base by 8% this year.

5. Income for the department will rise by at least 5% this year

➢ **How?**

New clients will directly add to Goal 1.

New clients will contribute financially to Goal 5.

Simultaneously maintaining current clients will help with both Goals 1 and 5.

Lever 1.3: IPBWA

In their improving performance by wandering around (see Key Idea 3) managers should have frequent discussions with all staff focused firmly on goals and outcomes as well as just methods for achieving them and tasks. Managers who have frequent contacts with their staff and have quality conversations about goals have been found to help performance improvements as well as supporting staff. Managers who help their staff connect to the big picture of the company strategy by talking to them will usually have a positive impact on performance.

Lever 1.4: Staff Recruitment and Selection

Standards and goals can be firmly communicated at the first opportunity of contact with staff which is during the recruitment and selection procedure.

Through the whole process, and in the documentation given to candidates, expected standards can be emphasised. This can cover both contractual standards (timekeeping, policies, diversity and equal opportunity issues etc) and softer behavioural and cultural standards (teamwork, customer care, support for colleagues, respect for people, etc), see Chapter 2, Key Idea 5.

We can also embed information about standards and goals in the work we do on job analysis, job description and person specification. You should be able to get help in this from your human resources department.

Lever 1.5: Induction

This is a further chance for managers to affirm standards and goals.

Specifically Lever 1.1 could be used effectively at this very early stage, a provisional goals and roles map could be worked through with the new staff member during their first week in post. This can be a very positive "start as you mean to go on" practice and can supply clarity and real support to staff.

Induction can also be used to clarify team culture and as a focus for high performance.

Lever 1.6: External Standards

Sometimes managers can use external competency frameworks and standards to help them set goals with their staff. Your staff development and human resources colleagues should be able to help here.

Lever 1.7: Culture

Build a culture in your team so that all staff frequently talk about goals and focus on their achievement as well as process and day to day fire fighting. Make a point, as a manager, to insert talk of specific outcomes and explicit goals in all of your conversations with staff, in both formal and informal contexts. For more ideas on this see Chapter 2, Key Idea 5 and some of the options for actions in issue 2 at the end of the book.

Lever 1.8: Role Modelling

Managers should strongly role model this focus on goals and standards. Role modelling by leaders has been found to have a substantial impact upon team members. So, as a manager, you could:

✓ Set and publicise your own goals.

✓ Behave to the standards that are set for the team.

✓ Discuss goals at every possible opportunity.

✓ Focus on outcomes.

✓ Spend time with team members setting goals.

Lever 1.9: Set Diversity Goals

In line with the policies and strategic goals of your organisation, all managers and staff should see fairness and diversity integrated into their day to day work. This should therefore be included in performance management, and specifically here, under goal setting.

There are also, of course, strong business reasons for paying attention to diversity. It can improve both individual and team/ departmental performance.

What Works 12: Lasting success

A huge piece of research by Buckingham and Coffman aimed at finding out what factors made a lasting successful organisation. The scale was large: covering 400 organisations, some 80,000 managers and about 1,000,000 employees.

The key finding was that the most important factor in lasting organisational success was the quality of management in these companies. More specifically it was to do with how well each manager engaged with each of their staff one to one. The more quality there was in that relationship, the more effective and successful the team/department/organisation would be.

Furthermore the research found 12 key factors that made up quality. These are framed as questions. The more positive the answer from each staff member, the better the manager is at managing and improving staff performance.

These questions were:

1. Were team members crystal clear about what was expected of them?
   Did the manager work with them to identify SMART goals?
   This is about the purpose and direction a manager will pass on to their staff.

2. Did team members get the materials and equipment needed to do the job well?
   Did the manager supply enough information and communication to the team member?

3. Did the manager play directly to each team member's strengths and work around weaknesses?
   Specifically, did the member of staff get the chance every day to do what they did best, what they were really good at?

4. Does the manager give sound, genuine recognition or praise to each team member?

5. Does the manager seem to care genuinely about staff?

6. Does the manager take each team member's professional and career development seriously, and do something real to help them achieve?

7. At work, did the opinions of team members count in a real, genuine way?

8. Does the organisation make team members feel their work was meaningful?
   Did everyone get good and understandable communication about the big picture?

9. Is every single member of the team committed to doing high quality work?
   Does the manager tackle poor performance and reward good performance?
   Does the manager do sensible connections?

10. Does each member of the team have someone at work who they can go to for confidential advice? This can be a mark of a supportive culture in the team.

11. At least twice a year, does the manager really engage with each and every team member about their overall progress and goals for the next year, their personal strategy? This connects to appraisal and the performance management delivery system, see Key Idea 3, Chapter 2

12. Overall, each year, does each team member have the opportunities to learn and grow at work?

Remember that these factors were firmly connected to organisational success, and for most of the companies in the research this meant financial success in competitive environments.

Also this research reinforced that a key factor in effective management is a strong, persistent focus on goals and outcomes.

Exercise and action planning: Assessing success

Do you think this research (see What Works 12: lasting success) has anything to offer you, your staff and your Business? If so, how? If not, why not?

....

....

Go through the 12 points above for your team. How well do you think you might score on each on a scale of 1-5? With 5 being performing excellently and 1 meaning there are multiple problems. If you wish, you could actually ask some team members themselves these questions about your leadership. This would certainly and positively demonstrate your personal commitment to receiving feedback and self development.

		1	2	3	4	5
1	Clear about goals	☹	○	😐	○	☺
2	Enough equip / info	☹	○	😐	○	☺
3	Do what best at	☹	○	😐	○	☺
4	Recognition, praise	☹	○	😐	○	☺
5	Care for staff	☹	○	😐	○	☺
6	Career development	☹	○	😐	○	☺
7	Opinions count	☹	○	😐	○	☺
8	Meaningful/big picture	☹	○	😐	○	☺
9	Committed to quality	☹	○	😐	○	☺
10	Supportive culture	☹	○	😐	○	☺
11	Engage in progress	☹	○	😐	○	☺
12	Opportunity to grow	☹	○	😐	○	☺

Overall, how might you score?

	1	2	3	4	5
Overall	☹	○	😐	○	☺

Notes on the 12 questions:

Based on this, are there any action points that you want to pursue?

Lever 1.10: Rule of Top 3 Goals

This can be an effective, straightforward and rough and ready tool that we can use in dealing with staff performance.

There is some theoretical grounding in this lever, though it is in essence practical and real world. The psychologist George Miller researched people's short term memory and the "rule of 6's and 7's" was coined to describe this. Miller indicated that most of us can only carry up to five to seven ideas in our minds at any one time. In using this lever we want each team member to carry their current priorities round with them, in their heads, so that it helps them to structure their time, focus their attention, ward off distractions and therefore maintain and improve their performance.

Now if we can only hold 7 ideas in our mind at once, we need to have space to think and make connections so if we reduce the 7 to 3 or 4 goals it will give added focus to our goal setting and achievement.

Basically this lever involves:

➢ You and your team member working out, "What are the top 3 goals that need to be achieved over the next three months/month/week/day/any relevant short term period?"

➢ This can prompt a quality conversation with your member of staff- taking into account the big picture for the team and the organisation, usually a good thing to do (see Lever 1.2). This process can force both the manager and their staff members to think deeply about what is going on and to come up with an agreed response that is both strategic and tactical.

➢ This lever can be particularly useful in a team or a company going through rapid change in a turbulent environment, for example changes to the business, major staff turnover, crises and unforeseen business opportunities.

➢ We can use this method with staff anywhere along the continuum, from the excellent performers through to ones who are struggling. The top performers can be given a very challenging set of goals, usually on a weekly or monthly basis. It can be used with poor performers to help you get a close grip on what they are doing, give them real focus and clarity. In desperate situations, calling for close management of a staff member and quick turnaround in their performance, this top 3 goals approach can even be used on a daily basis. It can sometimes work to help rescue what may seem like a hopeless situation.

➢ You sometimes need to be flexible by perhaps expanding this to the top 5 goals, but Miller's law would suggest that you do not go much higher than this. We want the team member to actually keep these priorities in their head, rather that just on paper, and to use them to guide what they do in their role on an almost minute by minute basis- another example of focus. If we work with 10, 15, 20 goals we run the risk of a wipeout, the staff member (especially the already poor performers) can freeze and even go backwards in performance and achievement.

➢ Of course the world of work is not this simple. Even excellent performers will have to spend time on issues that are outside their top 3 goals at some points, we have to be flexible and use common sense, for example in dealing with emergencies. Nevertheless, many managers find that this lever can add significantly to staff focus and performance.

An example, from a small law firm undergoing rapid expansion, new business initiatives, the departure of a key member of staff, new staff coming in and a raft of other issues at the same time.

Personal top goals to tackle over the next three months

Managing Partner
1. Develop new mindsets, ongoing basis, to cope with changes in the strategic environment
2. Work on new internal processes- to cope with goal 1
3. Business development facing outwards from the firm
4. Effective confidence building throughout the firm and externally

Lawyer 1
1. Develop more confidence in dealing with team and outside the firm, sell better.
2. Keep the daily maintenance tasks going strong.
3. Successfully implement the new software for work tracking, needs to be up and running in three months time.

Lawyer 2
1. Get stability in the team, staff and procedures.
2. Get more work in.
3. Get more profitable.

Outgoing lawyer
1. Manage the transition sensibly and effectively.
2. Continue to bring in money right up to departure and set up work for successor
3. Set up locum work (very specific projects for specific periods) after departure.

Office Manager
1. Project manage new internal processes effectively and quickly.
2. Focus on quick, effective recruitment.
3. Continue to focus on marketing the firm, particularly with the press.
4. Performance manage the support team effectively, supportively and closely.

New Lawyer 1
1. Hit the ground running re bringing money in.
2. Quick turnover of work.
3. Start work on role as long term go-getter.

New lawyer 2
1. Get to grips with caseload straight away.
2. Make money straight away.
3. Start to learn to be a go-getter.

New lawyer 3
1. Solid legal work after settling in and learning the ropes (first month).
2. Then immediately start making money.

New Trainee
1. Concentrate on precise/accurate work.
2. Effective marketing project work in tandem with the office manager.
3. Effective and efficient workload management.

Outside Consultant
1. Progress specific project, significant progress needed.
2. Support and mentor managing partner.
3. In consultation with managing partner produce three year strategic plan for the firm as well as first steps to this taking off.

As you can see, these are not necessarily SMART goals and we can use some flexibility around the number. They are, though, real and practical and help with focus and managing deep and rapid individual and organisational change.

Exercise and action planning: Understanding of goals

Review your goal and standard setting with your team. Does each member of your team know explicitly what goals they have to achieve over the next 12 months?

....
....
....

Does each member of your team have a clear understanding of the standards of behaviour that are expected of them and what these mean in their day to day work?

....
....
....

What levers do you need to action to improve your own practice in this area?

....
....
....

What support do you need from your manager and your organisation to progress in this?

....
....
....

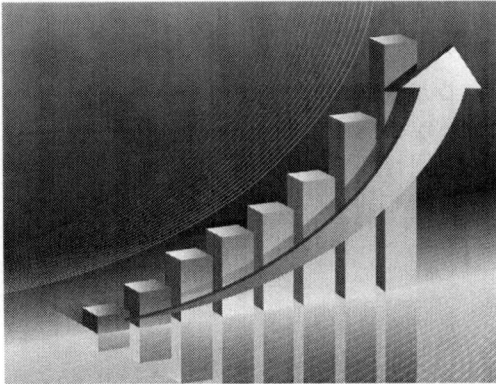

Step 2:
Measure staff performance

Levers in step 2:

2.1 The role of number crunching in performance management.

2.2 Just ask - straightforward is best.

2.3 Reprise of IPBWA

2.4 Modelling sound performance management

2.5 Using technology

2.6 Self monitoring by staff, team members tracking and changing their own performance.

2.7 Getting some HR help.

2.8 Documenting evidence, write things down!

2.9 Objectivity, relying on data, not subjectivity, in evaluating performance.

With robust standards and goals in place for all staff, we now need to think about how we track their achievement and measure their performance.

Managers should know fairly accurately, pretty much all of the time, where each member of their team is on the A to Z continuum (see Chapter 2, Key Idea 2).

We can also use Key Idea 3, the performance improvement delivery system, and Key Idea 4, the performance improvement habit, to gather information about team members' performances.

What Works 13: Performance management routine

One large piece of research around what makes an effective organisation, rather than talking about appraisal and supervision, indicated that a 'performance management routine' was important.

An effective performance management routine:

1. Is as simple and straightforward as it can be, this includes any documentation.

2. Encourages frequent interactions between a manager and each member of their team, multiple contact opportunities give the manager chance to gather data on that staff member's performance as well as influencing it positively.

3. Looked back at that team member's performance and learnt from it.

4. Looked forward to set good, SMART goals for the future.

5. Requires each team member to track their own performance and to be responsible, as much as possible, for their own performance management.

(See Buckingham and Coffman)

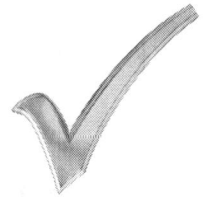

We need to remember that in measuring staff performances:

> We are looking for evidence of all performance, from poor to excellent (see Key Idea 2, in chapter 2), and not just focusing on sub-standard performance.

> The aim of this step, measuring performance, is not to punish or just accuse staff who are not performing. Nor is the aim to discipline staff or just to collect evidence for this purpose. Rather, the important goal is to continuously improve all staffs' work performances, to get a team member as close to Z as possible (see Key Idea 2).

> Only by collecting evidence continuously can we both tackle poor performance before it becomes severe as well as rewarding good performance.

Lever 2.1: Number Crunching

Firstly, number crunching - picking up hard data from various sources. This can be data about unit/departmental performance and then making a judgement about how an individual team member contributes to this. We can also try for data that tells us something directly about an individual's performance, eg paper feedback from customers.

Lever 2.2: Ask Customers/Users/Clients

A specific Lever would be to positively engage with their unit/ department's customers to get feedback. A proactive approach to this is a good idea, looking for good as well as problematic performance. Reactive ways of doing this usually just produce complaints and we get an unbalanced view of performance.

Lever 2.3: IPBWA

Improving performance by wandering around (see Key Idea 3) is an important way for managers to gather evidence of staff performance. They can do this by engaging directly with various staff members, by observing them at work, by meeting customers face to face etc.

A lot of good, soft evidence can be collected through this method. By this I mean that a manager can get a view of team culture, how staff engage with each other and with customers on a daily basis, how problems are solved (or not) and how much day by day excellent work performance is seen as important.

Lever 2.4: Role Modelling

The manager can have a powerful effect through their own willingness to collect data about their own management performance. This would, crucially, include positively seeking feedback from their own team.

Lever 2.5: IT and MIS

It is important to build IT and management information systems (MIS) that help us quickly collect data on collective and individual performance. Good systems should provide managers with up to date information, that they can then use to make judgements and then help team members to continuously improve their performance.

Lever 2.6: Self-Monitoring

Some research indicates that a very effective way of measuring performance is for team members to self-monitor, to track their own performance. This will be linked directly to a manager building a powerful performance management culture (see Key Idea 5).

Lever 2.7: HR Help

Most organisations' human resources departments can also help managers to develop ways to measure staff members' performance.

Lever 2.8: Record, always write things down

We should also remember that, if we are possibly measuring performance that is well below standard, then we always need to document. This can then serve as evidence in case the situation does result in some form of disciplinary action.

Lever 2.9: Objectivity

Managers need to be sure that they are objective in measuring staff performance and not let personal prejudice or unfair bias come into this.

Furthermore one of the criteria or goals that managers should measure staff against is how far they are achieving the company's commitment to treating people fairly and with respect.

Your organisation's human resources department should, again, help on this issue.

What Works 14: Scorecards

A common way to measure organisational performance is the balanced scorecard, Kaplan and Norton are key in pioneering this model.

Some organisations, trying to get a consistent, comprehensive, connected and effective way of managing and connecting company, department, team and individual performance, have used a version of this. Roughly, this will try to form a set of metrics by which we can track performance, usually under four headings:

➤ Customer service

➤ Financial

➤ Internal work processes

➤ Innovation and Learning

A manager can use this framework to form goals for each of these and then, over time, track these.

You can think about how some form of rough and ready framework, customised for your team and, indeed, for individual members of the team doing different jobs could help you get a grip on measuring each team member's performance. The clarity of this approach might also even help in encouraging individual staff to enthusiastically pursue and track their own performance.

Exercise and action planning:
Review of team member's performance

Review how you measure your team members' performances, do you know accurately how they are doing most of the time- do you know where they on the A to Z continuum (see Key Idea 2).

Note down your action points for the Levers 2.1 to 2.9

Step 3: Analyse and Understand Team Members' Performance

Levers in step 3:

3.1   Using the performance management delivery system.

3.2   Figuring out the reason why things happen.

3.3   Taking diversity issues into account

3.4   Using the C7 framework for finding out what's going on.

3.5   The QQRTPS model for dealing with performance issues.

This stage requires managers to think about the performance of each of their team members, to compare their actual performance on the job (Step 2) to the goals and standards that were set with them (Step 1) and then, essentially working out why, finding the drivers and explanations for each staff member's performance. In other words, moving on from "What's going on?" to "Why is this happening?"

Both managers and staff members need to:

✓ Understand the causes of sub-standard performance so that we can help staff to improve.

✓ Understand why some staff members perform excellently, so that they can continue to achieve this.

✓ Transfer the lessons learnt about individual performance, both across to other team members and, if possible, across the team and company.

✓ Understand the lessons from research about what works in improving performance.

Managers really need to use their judgement and analysis, and to make hard decisions. Staff rarely move from good performance to poor performance quickly. Managers need to measure performance (Step 2) continuously, pick up early signs of a downturn, understand why it is happening (if possible in consultation with the staff member themselves) and then move to action (Step 4).

Managers should consider their approach to diversity here. Is the team member's performance poor, or is it just different, or is the manager being subjective rather than objective? There is a tendency, well known by personnel experts, for managers to recruit staff who have the same background and work styles as themselves. They may recruit staff based on acceptability (will they fit in here and are they the same as us) rather than suitability (do they have the best skills for the role). This tendency can expand to how managers might measure staff performance and how they might manage staff on a day to day basis.

Effective organisations have a rich diversity of staff who have different styles, different ways of achieving goals. Excellent performance management actually drives diversity and equal opportunities. Poor or non-existent performance management can allow for unfair, subjective treatment of some staff. A well planned and implemented delivery system (see Key Idea 3) means that high performing staff are recognised and rewarded. Evaluation and reward are done on reasonably objective grounds rather than based on "is she/he one of us?" or "do they fit in here?" Staff who are different and, possibly, challenging to manage can be very effective and successful. Managers doing good performance management will recognise this and work with them positively.

Lever 3.1: Delivery System

Use the performance management delivery system (see Key Idea 3). The key points here are:

➢ Managers who engage frequently and genuinely with their staff should understand them better. Consequently they will be more able to really understand the roots of staff performance, tackle performance dips quickly and even predict and avoid downturns. For instance, it may be that a member of staff does not cope well with crises, thinking on their feet, situations. A good manager will know that this person will need extra support and help at certain times of the year, when the business is under pressure. This is performance improvement by wandering around.

➢ Regular supervision will also help a manager keep in touch with their staff, understand them better and head off performance dips, help them to improve performance and keep top performers interested and motivated.

➢ Finally, the appraisal interview gives an opportunity to explore deeply, and over a long term, with each individual member of staff what motivates them and how the manager can support this.

What Works 15: Emotional intelligence

Recent research about effective leadership has used the term emotional intelligence. This has been found to be an essential building block for managers.

It highlights that emotionally intelligent managers:

➢ Have an insight into and awareness of their own emotional states at work.

➢ Have an understanding of and can empathise with the emotional states of their colleagues.

➢ Customise their leadership behaviour styles for different staff over a range of situations,

➢ Become very effective managers, leaders who get real, long term results and drive successful teams and organisations.

Furthermore there are competencies that underlie this emotional intelligence, and these can be developed. We can learn to become more emotionally intelligent

This research is extensive, see Daniel Goleman's and Martyn Newman's work.

Your human resources and staff development departments can probably help you look further into this area.

Exercise and action planning:
Brainstorm on staff performance levels

In your experience-

Brainstorm reasons why some staff perform consistently excellently.
Prioritise: What do you think are the key reasons?

....

....

....

....

Brainstorm reasons why some staff can perform poorly.
Prioritise: What do you think are the key reasons?

....

....

....

....

Brainstorm reasons why some staff perform averagely.
Prioritise: What do you think are the key reasons?

....

....

....

....

....

....

Lever 3.2: Reasons Why Staff Perform Differently

Some common reasons given for staff performance, good and poor, are given here but there are thousands more.

Motivational:
➢ Lack of motivation
➢ They don't know why they should perform well
➢ "Naturally" motivated
➢ They are not committed
➢ Self starter
➢ They are self motivated- "they will always do well"
➢ They are committed
➢ They enjoy succeeding
➢ They are cynical and whinging
➢ They like a challenge
➢ They are achievement orientated
➢ They are proud of what they do and achieve
➢ They are really interested in what they do
➢ They get satisfaction from doing a good job
➢ They are bored

Knowledge of what is expected
➢ They don't know what to do
➢ They don't know how to perform
➢ They have not been developed
➢ They have unclear goals and expectations
➢ They have clear goals and expectations

Personal difficulties:
➢ Reasons outside work, difficulties in their private life
➢ Life/work balance issues
➢ Money
➢ They are off sick

Workload management:
➢ They simply have too much work, it is impossible for them to do well across the whole of their role
➢ They are simply incapable
➢ They are lazy
➢ They are natural hard workers

Relationships at work:
- They "don't get on" with their manager.
- They are being bullied
- They are not supported by their colleagues.
- Their manager is terrible
- Their manager is excellent
- They are reliant upon other people, who either give them a great service or, alternatively a hopeless one
- They are naturally awkward
- They are/are not communicated with

Attitude:
- They have strong values
- They are not effective
- They are not rewarded
- They feel rewarded
- They are rebellious
- They are not proud of what they do, it doesn't matter how hard they work they always do a poor job
- They perform badly because they can
- Habits (good and bad), sometimes developed over years

The organisation:
- The organisation provides them with the tools to do the job
- They believe in the organisation
- They don't like the direction the organisation is going
- They trust the organisation
- They role model their manager
- They don't trust the organisation
- They are just sound people
- The IT provided helps them or lets them down
- Our structure and processes

Etc, etc ...

As can be seen, there are very many reasons behind why staff perform as they do, and the pattern is probably different for each individual. In the next step we will identify actions managers can take to tackle these issues.

Lever 3.3: Understanding Diversity

In analysing the reasons for performance differences all managers should take account of the possible impact of unfair treatment, bullying and possible institutional discrimination. This is an essential step before a manager moves on to action.

Your human resources and staff development departments should be able to help here.

The next few Levers are rough and ready models that managers can use to try to understand 'What's going on' in their team.

Lever 3.4: The C7 Model

Faced with poor performance, this is a rule of thumb analysis a manager can use to start to get a grip on what is going on, why it is happening and what they can do about it. It requires you to use your judgement, even take a chance and possibly make some hard decisions.

Basically we try to answer which one or more of these factors are relevant for a particular member of staff and their performance issues:

- ➢ Competence
- ➢ Capacity
- ➢ Capability
- ➢ Confidence
- ➢ Culture
- ➢ Corporate
- ➢ Commitment

> **Competence:**

This is the team member not performing because they simply do not, at the moment, have the right skills and knowledge or do not have them to the required level.

The response to this is some form of staff development for that individual.

> **Capacity:**

As a manager we always have to think about capacity. It looks closely at the issue: "Is this team member not performing up to standard because I am giving them too much work to do- no one at their level could get through that much?"

The response to this is to work with them on reducing workload, the onus here is on the manager taking responsibility.

Conversely people can actually under-perform when they are not up to capacity because they are not being challenged.

> **Capability:**

The person is not performing to the right level and we think that they never will. They simply do not have and can never acquire the correct level of skills and knowledge whatever we do to help them.

If this is the reason for gross under-performance then our response as a manager is tough: we need to get them out of this job, into another one that they are capable of or dismiss them.

The lesson for managers and businesses, if this happens, is that we should not have taken this person on to do this job in the first place. It is a recruitment and selection issue. Indeed, excellent recruitment and selection is the first and vital step in effective performance management.

> ➤ **Confidence:**

This can be a subtle issue. You think this person has the right amount of work and has the right skills and knowledge but for some puzzling reason does not seem to be able to achieve their performance goals at the moment. It may be that their confidence has, for some reason, dipped. Managers can help here, working with the person to rebuild their confidence, perhaps getting to the reason why this has happened and how we can support the team member to get back on their feet again.

Sometimes this downturn is a result of issues outside work. The problem here can be twofold. Firstly, what if we cannot rebuild confidence and performance continues to be unsuccessful? Secondly, connected to this, how long can we let this go on for before we have to treat this as if it was a capability issue?

In tough times, when businesses are in competitive environments, this can be a difficult dilemma for a manager. One response seems to be important here, always set clear, explicit deadlines for a return to acceptable performance for a member of staff, never let the issue continue without some form of timetable.

> ➤ **Culture:**

This is another difficult issue for a manager to admit, especially if they have been in charge of their team for some time. When this is relevant, it means that the team culture in some ways impacts negatively on collective and individual performance. This downturn can be because individual team members are not supported by their colleagues, or that the atmosphere in the team is so toxic and poisonous that team members cannot perform well, or that performance is inhibited in some way because the team climate lacks the positive aspects that form a high performance culture.

At its extreme it can mean that an individual is pressurised or even bullied into low performance. In my experience this is rare, thankfully. However, I do remember an example given to me by a client some years ago. He had at one time worked in a factory and was forcibly warned about working quickly, the culture was a clear one of slow and slipshod work performance.

What all of these strands have in common is that the responsibility is clear, the manager must tackle the culture in their team as it is a key part of their job. More positively, shaping a high performance culture in your team can produce uplifts in individual and collective performances- see Key Idea 5.

➤ **Corporate**

This would mean that the systems, policies, procedures, communication, machinery and technology support from other units and the structure of the organisation is so bad, so unhelpful, that even very competent, committed and capable staff can't do a good job however hard they work. The root of individual and collective poor performance is systemic. When this happens it is serious, possibly terminal for the company and requires radical and deep action at organisational and not individual level. This possibility needs to be mentioned here and considered by managers, but this book does not cover the remedies required; this is a serious organisational performance issue.

➤ **Commitment:**

This is the trickiest of the 7 Cs to deal with. Here the sub-standard performance is not connected to competence, capability or confidence. The team member certainly seems to have the skills and knowledge needed, they are qualified for the role. Furthermore they do not seem to be suffering from some temporary confidence drop. Nor is it a capacity issue, they have the same, correct amount of work that their peers achieve smoothly. They might, however, claim that their performance issue is a capacity issue, you have given them too much work! Everyone else in the team is doing an excellent job, the culture is good and supports excellence. Furthermore there are no organisational reasons for low performance.

Under this commitment banner we are heading towards the conclusion that the team member has decided that they are simply not going to perform, not going to work as hard as their colleagues. For whatever range of reasons they have decided to place themselves very firmly at the A end of the performance line in Key Idea 2.

This can be immensely difficult to respond to as a manager. For a start you have to work your way systematically through the other 6 Cs before you can safely come to this conclusion. Furthermore, from a human resources point of view, you will need to leave a laborious and comprehensive paper trail of your efforts at discounting the first 6 Cs. Also, dealing with this issue means you are, in effect, telling a member of staff who has decided to not work properly that they must raise their performance or else you'll take dire actions; a charged, possibly emotional and challenging piece of leadership even for an experienced manager.

There may be a number of reasons why someone will decide to not work properly. The team member may not realise that their standard of performance is unacceptable. The manager, then, needs to deal assertively and clearly with this.

The person may perform at their unacceptably low level "because they can"- in other words that have been doing this for years and no one has tackled them on it so they believe themselves to be invulnerable.

Key points here are:

➢ Never do nothing- the situation will always get worse.

➢ Never do nothing- this situation will poison the team culture, demoralise the other members of the team and probably produce further performance issues or possibly result in your good performers going elsewhere, see Key Idea 1.

➢ Always get support from your manager and your organisation's human resources department.

➢ Expect that sorting this out will take a long time.

➢ Then grasp the nettle and take firm action.

➢ Acknowledging that one conclusion could be that this person is dismissed, even though this is not your goal as a manager.

➢ Your clear objective is to get this person to raise their performance to an acceptable level and not relapse.

Lever 3.5: QQRTPS

This is another rough and ready model managers can use to get some understanding of aspects of both poor and excellent performance. The framework can be explicitly used when you meet with your staff members to discuss performance. You need to go through each of the strands, evaluating and then identifying options for action.

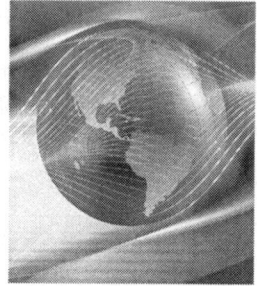

QQRTPS stands for:

➢ Quality

➢ Quantity

➢ Resources

➢ Time

➢ Pace

➢ Scope

Achieving appropriate levels of QQRTPS in a role can signify good performance. These individual aspects are not independent they interact together, so that it is important for a manager to consider, together with the team member, all of these.

What we do is collect the data from Step 2 and then look at:

➤ **Quality:**
How well is the team member achieving the quality standards that we have set for their role?

For example, this could be around accuracy for someone inputting data, the number of client complaints for someone providing a service, the reputation of new clients brought to the firm or the "production" values for a staff member doing forms of technical work.

Getting at what quality actually means is usually difficult and open to interpretation. However, it is often crucial. For example, an IT professional may have high technical skills in problem solving hardware and software issues. This aspect of quality can be relatively easy to measure. A crucial part of their job can be how well they communicate with people outside of their own speciality. This aspect of quality is more ambiguous but essential to high performance in role. Therefore the team member and manager need to clarify what this aspect of quality actually means in practice. For many parts of many jobs the best way to approach this is talking. The manager and team member need to discuss what quality in that role means to them and then reach some form of shared understanding on how to measure it.

If there is a deficit here then the usual response would be to catch any shortfall as soon as possible. Identifying quality of work as an issue can give the team member and manager a focus for action to improve performance.

> **Quantity:**

How much work is the staff member achieving?

Note that quantity of work is not an independent issue for a team member. Clearly we have to also take into account the other aspects of QQRTPS- particularly the quality of the work done, the pace of work, how many resources they need for a particular project, did they achieve the deadline or time for specific tasks and was what they did the right thing to do, was it within the scope of their role.

For some roles in some organisations measuring the quantity of work someone does is straightforward, how many things did someone make, how many tapes did a support staff member word process etc. However, in some roles it can be more difficult calculating how many meetings a staff member attended may not be very helpful. The quantity may be high, "I have been to six meetings today" or "I have been in contact with 11 clients today," but what about the quality?

Here a manager might find it useful to always think beyond mere "numbers" and engage with a staff member about

✓ Outputs

✓ Outcomes

✓ Personal Impacts,

to nudge the discussion toward quality.

For example: You went to six meetings yesterday, can we talk about:

Outputs: What came out of these meetings?

Outcome: What effect do you think these meetings will have on your performance and team performance?

Personal Impact: How do you think you personally contributed to the meetings?

So while we always need to take sheer quantity of work into account when analysing performance, managers also need to be more subtle in their analysis and discussions with staff and bring in other more sophisticated aspects of their work.

➢ **Resources:**

Is a team member giving the appropriate amount of resources to a particular project/goal/task that is part of their role and therefore contributes to their performance level?

I am using resources here to cover a number of things, principally the team member's time but this can also include their energy, concentration, or their budget. Over resourcing a specific task can drive up quality achievement for that project and give the appearance of top performance. However, using resources inappropriately like this can mean that other aspects of that person's role can suffer. For this reason managers should try to look at a staff member's performance across their entire role.

➢ **Time or deadline:**

Did your team member succeed at a deadline for a specific project/goal/task?

This just gives us another way to look at performance. As with the other aspects of this tool we can use it to analyse both excellent and below standard performance and to move on to working out options for action for that member of staff. Remember, all of the strands of this rough and ready tool connect with all of the others. We have to look at every one of them. For example, a team member may consistently make deadlines on all of their work but there may be issues with quality of performance and with the resources they use to achieve this. Alternatively, they may make time deadlines only with a proportion of their work, so the quantity of overall work is insufficient.

➢ **Pace:**
Put simply, does the staff member work fast enough?

Again we can see that we cannot think about this issue without considering all of the others, for example someone may work very fast, produce a high quantity of things but the quality is inappropriate for the business they are in. Furthermore, pace may be hard to judge. We usually cannot tell by the person's velocity around the workplace! Usually we get at this by noticing the quantity of the work that staff member does and whether they hit time deadlines.

➢ **Scope:**
Is the team member doing the right things, are they doing things that they should not be doing that are outside their role?

A staff member doing the wrong things, doing tasks that are outside their job, usually means that there are essential parts of their role that do not get done. Sometimes, this means that they are spending their time doing things below their pay level because they are easy, whilst their proper and more difficult tasks are left undone.

Managers need to be careful here:

➢ Have we helped the team member by fully clarifying their role with them, communicating and supporting?

➢ If we take this issue of scope too far then we can stifle independence. We do want staff to use their initiative and to sometimes, particularly in a serious crisis, to sort things out even if it may entail them doing tasks that are outside their usual role.

We can use QQRTPS to focus on performance with staff. It can be a rough and ready tool that we can keep in our heads and use in real life in a range of performance situations, jumping about between the ingredients, working with the staff member to get a grip on what is going on and then taking action.

Someone with commitment issues (see Lever 3.4) may try to use aspects of this model to obscure or falsely account for their poor performance. "What do you mean, not good enough, look how fast I'm working?" or "What do you mean, not good enough quality, look at how much I do?" etc. Remember, we need to look at all of the QQRTPS model to make sense of performance.

Consistent top performance across all of QQRTPS indicates a real top performer- they achieve the correct quality standards, do more than enough work without wasting any resources, always achieve time deadlines, work fast and do the right things. Furthermore, they will learn from this success as much as others can sometimes learn from failure.

Exercise and action planning: Performance issues

Think of some performance issues you have had to tackle, or that you are dealing with now. These can cover anything, from poor performance to excellent performance.

....

....

....

....

....

Experiment- use Levers 3.4 and 3.5 to try to make sense of them and to identify some real options for action.

....

....

....

....

....

....

Step 4:
Take Action

Levers in step 4:

4.1   Plan, plan, plan, plan.....

4.2   Leadership and performance management.

4.3   The role of rewards and motivation.

4.4   Again, IPBWA

4.5   Using feedback effectively

4.6   Goal setting and performance management.

4.7   Reprising the role of strategy, the "big picture" in performance management.

4.8   Effective communication and performance issues.

4.9   Staff development and training.

4.10 The power of expectations and self fulfilling prophecies in performance management.

4.11 Building a sound platform for performance.

4.12 Once again, role modelling by a manager.

4.13 Using policies and procedures effectively.

4.14 Discipline and dismissal.

4.15 Building confidence in staff, effective support for team members.

4.16 Using process effectively, using inquiry rather than advocacy.

4.17 The FCSC framework- focus/control/sense of urgency/clarity.

In this step managers take leadership actions to improve performance. Remember that the model outlined here in this book is cumulative. We need to work on the Key Ideas, then set goals and standards, measure staff performance and really try to understand and analyse the factors that can cause performance across the whole of the A to Z continuum. Only then should managers take action.

Particular care should be taken if you are tackling poor performance and you might, at some point, have to take disciplinary action. You need to really understand your company's employment policies and procedures as well as some idea of the relevant legislation. The best thing to do always is to consult with your human resources department as soon as possible. If this is not possible, try for a friendly employment lawyer.

Care should also be taken that you are managing fairly and that any action you take is based on good, sound evidence and not assumptions or ideas about one right way.

Remember here that previous levers, particularly those in Step 3, all have relevance here. They could have been included under both sections. For instance Levers 3.4 and 3.5 above can certainly help a manager and staff member to understand better what is going on, to analyse, but also crucially can get us involved in identifying options for action and then implementing our plans.

Everything we have done so far then leads us to Step 4, doing something. This can range from, what can we do to raise a staff member's unacceptable level of performance to taking steps to make sure that a top performer stays motivated and presses on to even better things.

Lever 4.1: Planning Interventions

Based on the causes of performance (see Step 3) managers should be clever and organised about the actions they take. Use the same care and attention, for example, that you might take in planning a business project. Strengthen this by taking clear, well thought out, intelligent, decisions with supporting well documented action plans.

Two examples:

In dealing with a member of staff who has shown a sudden decline in performance because of some domestic, private difficulty:

➢ Be supportive, if you deal sensitively now with this team member and positively help them tackle their temporary problems then they will repay you in the long term in their commitment, motivation and flexibility in the future.

➢ Be careful about intervening in private areas of a team member's life. Even if you think that their performance dip is because of external factors, the team member can legitimately choose not to discuss these with you. In this case you can still offer help from your organisation (for example counselling where available and appropriate).

➢ Be as flexible as you can in dealing with this matter. Research indicates that, in general, staff value and respond to flexibility. In situations of difficulty they will value this even more.

➢ Use teamwork where appropriate. Without breaching confidentiality other members of the team can support the member of staff and fill in temporarily for their performance shortfall. This, in the long term, can also help teamwork.

> Nevertheless, your company still needs to think about the business and providing a competitive, excellent service to customers. Therefore, the team member should not be given an open ended plan. Write in explicit dates and times for review. A team member can sometimes be given some form of compassionate leave or flexibility to deal with a problem. However this should always be carefully reviewed, say, on a weekly basis, at a particular day, time and place. At this review, a further explicit plan should be drawn up.

> Always document these plans. This is good practice and not just to cover your back. It means that the team member knows where they stand and has a good structure for returning to good performance standards.

> Make sure that your plans are in line with your organisation's policies- always consult with human resources for advice about this, or get help from an employment lawyer.

Managing a high achieving, innovative staff member:

> They will have a heavy workload. If you want to help them initiate new innovative projects then this will require careful planning so that they can keep a reasonable life/work balance and not burn out in the long term.

> Other members of your team may have some capacity to take over some of this person's workload. Indeed this could actually also add to their professional development. Performance management by you across the team (using the delivery system, Key Idea 3) can help you do this in an organised, sensible way.

> Helping the team member set good, SMART goals for this Key Role (see Lever 1.1) will contribute to their success.

> As a team manager you could also plan how the innovative work and learning that this particular team member is driving could be spread across other team members (and perhaps across the company).

> Again documenting this plan can help you and the team member keep on top of it, make sure that it is successful.

Remember- In planning for performance improvement:

➤ All plans for performance improvement should build on the goals and standards set out in Step 1 of this model, use the evidence from Step 2 and be informed by the understanding and analysis from Step 3.

➤ Recovery plans for staff whose performance is below standard should always be fully documented and dated and shown to the particular staff member in case this ends in a disciplinary hearing.

If in any doubt, contact your human resources people or a relevant lawyer.

Exercise and action planning: Planning for performance improvement

Review the way that you plan for performance improvement for your team.

How might you want to change/improve this?

Lever 4.2: Provide excellent leadership

This is wider than performance management and this book. Excellent and continuously improving leadership will always contribute to individual staff continuously improving their own performance.

For example:

✓ Working on building your team/department's culture or climate. Having a strong, positive culture has been shown, in some research, to have a substantial impact, in some cases of about 30% to 40%, upon productivity in some manufacturing industries.

✓ Work on your own leadership styles- how you deal with your team and difficult situations. Again this has been found to impact positively on individual staff performance.

✓ Work on the team/departmental environment, ie. your structure, processes and systems. Improvements in these will lead to individual team member performance improvements.

✓ Work on how you manage change.

✓ As a leader, work on your emotional intelligence (see What Works 15).

What Works 16: The Hay model; engaged performance for excellence

In 2002 the Hay Group researched how organisations could motivate staff and therefore maintain and even improve on excellent performance.

Their conclusion was the notion of 'Engaged Performance', when staff were immersed in and enthusiastic about their work and involved in an implicit contract with the organisation where behaviours that drive the company forward are rewarded in some way.

They say disengaged employees:

"Go through the motions of what is required of them at work. They are not proactive, do not show either initiative or commitment, but most perform well enough to get by as acceptable (See Step 1 above- this is equivalent to achieving minimum standards but not pressing on further to progress goals)."

This research indicates there are six sets of factors that organisations and managers need to work on to get 'engaged employees'.

These are shown by:

1. **Quality of Work**
   - Perception of the value of the work they do, does it make a difference in some way?
   - How challenging and interesting is the work?
   - Real achievement opportunities
   - Relative freedom and autonomy in role.
   - Tough but reasonable workload
   - The quality of work relationships

2. **Work/Life Balance**
   - Supportive environment at the company
   - Recognition of life cycle needs/flexibility by the organisation and individual managers
   - Relative security of income
   - A good sociable environment

3. **Inspiration and Values**
    - High quality of leadership at all levels
    - Organisational values and behaviours
    - The reputation of the organisation
    - Risk sharing across the company- not an individual blame culture
    - Recognition for achievement and effort
    - Excellent communication across the organisation

4. **Enabling environment comprising**
    - Physical environment
    - Tools and equipment
    - Job training
    - Information and processes
    - Safety and personal security

5. **Future Growth/ Opportunity**
    - Learning and development opportunities beyond people's current job
    - Career advancement opportunities
    - Performance improvement as an ongoing aim
    - Feedback at all times

6. **Tangible Rewards comprising:**
    - Competitive pay
    - Good benefits
    - Incentives for higher and higher performance
    - Ownership potential
    - Recognition awards
    - Fairness of rewards across the business

Exercise and action planning: Using the Hay model

Many of the factors in the Hay Model start at an organisation wide level. However, there are local actions that managers might be able to take to improve staff performance.

Use the model to identify where you might improve your management performance.

....
....
....
....
....
....
....

Are there any messages for your business from this model?

....
....
....
....
....

How will you pass these messages on?

....
....
....
....
....

We must also remember that management action to improve performance at this step, based on careful analysis at Step 3, may not directly address that individual member of staff. Their under performance may in fact be due to external factors, and the manager should then focus on other targets that affect performance.

Examples would be:

❑ Do we have the right structure in the department/team?

❑ Do we have the right work processes and systems?

❑ Do we have enough resources?

❑ Do we have enough effective communication?

❑ Do we receive a good enough service from our colleagues in other teams/departments so that we can do a good job?

❑ Do we have the correct IT/technology?

❑ Do we have the right strategy?

❑ Do I, as manager, provide the best leadership?

In other words the corporate part of the 7 Cs model.

Exercise and action planning: Review of your leadership development

Based on what we have covered so far, review your own leadership development.

....

....

....

....

....

....

....

What specific leadership development goals do you have for the next 12 to 18 months?

....

....

....

....

....

....

....

How will these improve your staff's performance?

....

....

....

....

....

....

Lever 4.3: Rewarding and Motivating Staff

People are different to each other and are motivated by different things. The manager's job is to judge what these factors are for each member of staff.

However, there are some factors that seem to work very generally.

Some of these are:

✓ Having clear goals and knowing what is expected of you.

✓ Effective feedback.

✓ Recognition.

✓ Positive Attention.

✓ It also seems that most people also appreciate and are motivated by being at a flexible workplace, specifically in how the organisation helps with life/work balance.

✓ The meaningfulness of work, the chance to do a good job.

Exercise and action planning: Motivating staff

For each member of your team, identify what motivates them to continuously work on performance improvement.

....

....

....

....

....

....

Specifically, how do you motivate the high achievers?

....

....

....

....

....

....

On the other hand, what methods do you use to deal with the low performers?

....

....

....

....

....

....

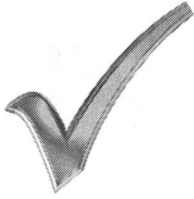

What Works 17: Hertzberg's motivational ideas

An American researcher, Frederick Hertzberg, wrote about motivation.

His key points were that:

➢ **There are hygiene or maintenance factors, such as:**
  • Pay
  • Conditions
  • Security
  • Physical environmental factors
  • Policies

These do not motivate staff in any positive way. They may persuade someone to work for one organisation rather than another. However, if these factors are not present then this will cause dissatisfaction and demotivation.

➢ **Then there are motivators, such as:**
  • Opportunity for career advance
  • Promotion
  • Growth
  • Development
  • Factors in the job itself
  • Recognition
  • Chances for achievement

These actually do make a difference to staff motivation and therefore to performance.

Some interesting things about this model are:

➢ How it treats money/pay - it says that it does not motivate staff. However, it may be that pay levels are a way that the organisation shows how much it values a member of staff.

➢ The hygiene and maintenance factors are sometimes out of the control of most managers in some companies, and cost money.

➢ However, the motivators are, to an extent, under a managers' control. This means that you can work with your team members to drive up these factors for them. From this point of view this can be seen as an optimistic, positive model.

Lever 4.4: Improving Performance by Wandering Around

We have already indicated that:

✓ Paying staff frequent, genuine and positive attention can motivate them to improve performance.

✓ Frequent interactions, if done sensibly and sensitively, can impact positively on staff performance and keep you in touch, as a manager, with what is going on at the front line.

✓ This also allows you to involve in one of the most effective and cheap ways of developing staff performance- coaching from their manager.

✓ By wandering around you will be in a position to give staff timely, real feedback. This is another cheap and effective way of improving performance.

Exercise and action planning: Wandering around

As as manager, do you get about enough, do you wander around? Think of ways in which you could improve this aspect of your performance and add these to your action plan.

Lever 4.5: Feedback

Effective feedback is one of the most effective, straightforward and cheap ways to improve staff performance.

Feedback is information given to staff members to help them maintain and improve their performance.

Feedback can be:

➢ Motivational: specific information given to a person about something they have just done well.

➢ Developmental: specific information given to a team member focused on how they can improve performance.

➢ A combination of both of these.

These will usually result in performance improvement.

Critical success factors for feedback:

- **Specific**- and not general (for example: not "you have to do better" but specific advice on exactly what needs improving)

- **Timely**- should be as close as possible to the incident etc that you are giving feedback on.

- **Actionable**- the discussion should move to what the team member can actually do to improve their behaviour.

- **Developmental**- suggesting ways in which the team member can learn from the incident.

- **Appropriately delivered** (pace and process)- take account of the understanding of the issues by the person and their emotional state.

- **Goal and outcomes focused**- this improves communication, letting the person know what exactly you want them to achieve rather than how they should accomplish it.

- **Objective behaviour based** (not attitude)- you need to focus on what the person did, not who they are, or what they might be thinking. This factor is also important to guard against unfair treatment of staff based on bias or discrimination.

- **Lodged in positive culture**- so that team members' feedback to each other (and to you, their manager) rather than just manager to team member.

- **Documented**- this is helpful to keep track of performance improvement and is particularly important if the staff member's performance is causing real worry and might lead to discipline.

What Works 18: Giving feedback

An important writer (Trevor Boutall) about management indicates how you can make the most of feedback.

Giving feedback checklist:

❑ Always seek opportunities to provide feedback to teams and individuals on their performance. Feedback can help people to understand if they are doing a good job or if there are areas in which they can improve and develop. Feedback can be given in any number of ways- formally or informally, in conversation or in writing.

❑ Choose the right, appropriate place and time to give feedback. Feedback is more useful and relevant if provided quickly. Sometimes it is appropriate to give feedback publicly, but often a quiet word with a member of your team is what is required.

❑ Always respond to and recognise good performance and achievement. Take opportunities to congratulate people.

❑ Provide constructive suggestions and encouragement for improving future performance. When people are not performing well, tell them and advise them how they can improve.

❑ Encourage people to self assess- ask open questions (eg. "How do you think the project went?") about how they see their own performance and then try to get them to be really specific.

❑ Provide feedback in detail and in a manner and at a level and pace which is appropriate to the people concerned.

❑ Encourage people to seek clarification, always check their understanding and give them the opportunity to ask questions.

❑ Encourage people to make suggestions on how things, systems and procedures for example, could be improved - their performance may be greatly improved by changes to procedures and working practices.

❑ Document details of any actions agreed.

❑ Review performance - check back at appropriate times to see whether performance has improved or been maintained.

What Works 19: The power of feedback

McCarty reported an experiment with students at a University.

➢ Group 1 were genuinely praised for all of the positive work they did on a series of projects.

➢ Group 2 were simply criticised for the things they did not do well.

➢ Group 3 received no feedback at all except for raw assignment marks.

In terms of improving performance, group 1 progressed tremendously. Groups 2 and 3 either stayed still in performance or deteriorated.

This research, connecting this and some other work, indicated that, "When organizations deprive employees of specific job-related information, they inhibit their performance."

There are strong reasons why managers often do not give feedback:

- They are too busy
- It's emotionally difficult- they can't deal with the team member's reaction
- They won't be liked
- They might be attacked
- The person will be upset
- There may be a confrontation
- They will be seen as a soft touch
- They will be seen as bullying
- They will be seen as nit-picking

Etc, etc .....

However, despite these there are powerful reasons for giving feedback to staff (if done effectively):

✓ In the long and medium (and sometimes short) term it will result in performance improvement

✓ It will improve communication

✓ It will motivate high performers

✓ It will help low performers to see practical ways in which they can improve

✓ It can help teamwork, high achievers see that low performers are being tackled; low performers will see the benefits of improving

✓ It is cheap, managers can do this as they are wandering around

✓ It can, over time, improve the professional relationship between team members and their manager

Lever 4.6: Goal Setting and Tracking

Along with feedback, goal setting is known to be a strong method for improving staff performance.

We covered numerous aspects of this under Step 1. However, it is worth noting again that managers who focus on goals and continuously amend, review and track their progress can have a powerful impact upon improving the performance of staff. Not least, this emphasis can help to clarify what the manager explicitly expects of staff, again thought to be a useful tool in performance improvement.

The goals and roles map, worked on in Step 1, would be a useful reference here.

Exercise and action planning: Clear idea of key goals

Carrying on from the work done in Step 1, does each member of your team have a clear idea of their key goals, what are the really important results they need to achieve this year?

....

....

....

....

If you are not convinced that this is the case, then what actions can you take?

....

....

....

....

Lever 4.7: Use the Big Picture and Strategy

Many studies indicate that most people want to see their own day to day work as meaningful, to see that it makes a difference. Managers can help staff, and therefore motivate them to improve performance, by working with them to make the connection between what they do every day and the overall purpose of their team/department/unit/business.

This means managers having a strong grasp of strategy, the big picture and using every opportunity they can to communicate this. For example:

➢ When they are wandering around

➢ At appraisals

➢ At supervision

➢ At team meetings

➢ At away days

➢ In written communication

➢ During planning meetings

➢ In professional discussions

➢ In coaching sessions

➢ In planning training and development

➢ During feedback

➢ In newsletters etc

Exercise and action planning: Strategic priorities

How clear are you about your organisation's strategic priorities?

....

....

....

Do you know how they fit into your team/unit/ department's strategic priorities?

....

....

....

How do you connect these to the work of each of your staff?

....

....

....

Do you need to improve in this area? Make some action points on how you will achieve the improvements.

....

....

....

....

....

....

Lever 4.8: Communication between manager and staff

This lever is important for a number of reasons:

> If a staff member does not know what they should be doing, then the manager needs to discuss this with them or provide clear documentation.

> If a team member does not know why they should be doing something then the manager needs to help them fit their goals and role into the big picture, to give them information. This can be done through appraisal (see Key Idea 3)

> If a staff member does not know how to do a task- then the manager needs to make sure they communicate properly with them.

> It demonstrates to the team member that their manager is paying positive attention to them (the Hawthorne Effect) and cares about them as a person (see What Works 12).

Exercise and action planning: Communication

List the ways in which you communicate with your team.

Overall is this communication effective?

Are there any gaps? Where?

What should you continue doing?

What should you stop doing?

What new ways of communication should you try out?

What extra skills do you need to develop?

Add these to your action plan.

Lever 4.9: Development and Training for Staff

This can be relevant when:

➢ The reason why a team member is not performing as expected is that they are unable to at the moment but have the potential to do so. In other words there is a skills and/or knowledge gap.

➢ When a team member wants to improve their skills or develop new ones so that they can build upon current good performance.

➢ The manager knows that there will be changes in the department/team that mean staff will need new skills in order to continue to perform well in the future.

➢ For the team member's own career development.

Lever 4.1 is relevant here, training and development interventions with staff need to be well planned, with:

➢ Specific goals

➢ Follow up

➢ Opportunity to practise new skills

➢ Support from the manager

➢ The most appropriate and effective type of development method

➢ If possible the method should be customised to the team member's learning style

➢ Careful evaluation

➢ Connection with the team/unit/department's strategy

➢ A strong connection with the team member's career strategy

Going on a training course is not the only method to train and develop staff; indeed it can be a very expensive one.

Methods of staff development open to a manager can be:

➢ One to one coaching (either by the manager or another team member or an external person)

➢ Problem solving and learning groups, with other staff, sometimes called action learning sets

➢ Mentoring

➢ Reading

➢ Taking a qualification

➢ Online

➢ Self study

➢ Training courses

The most powerful (and cheap) method of learning is when staff (and their manager) do continuous, conscious day to day learning from everyday life at work. In other words, staff get into the habit of learning everyday at work.

Managers can help them do this by using the Kolb Learning Cycle with staff.

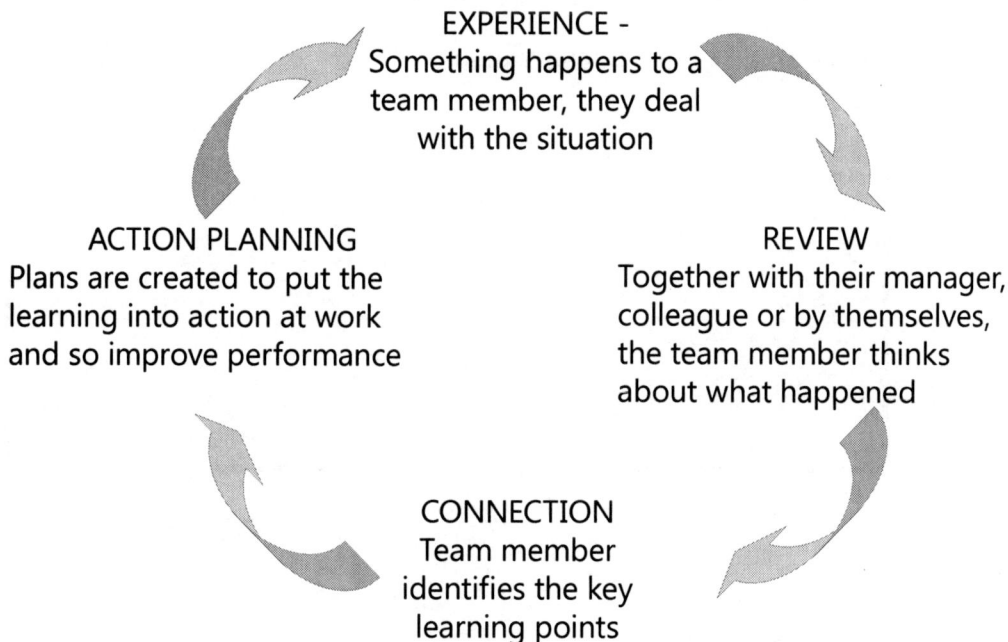

EXPERIENCE -
Something happens to a team member, they deal with the situation

REVIEW
Together with their manager, colleague or by themselves, the team member thinks about what happened

CONNECTION
Team member identifies the key learning points

ACTION PLANNING
Plans are created to put the learning into action at work and so improve performance

This model can be used to frame feedback to staff, starting at experience, then moving round clockwise. It firmly links feedback to learning and gives an opportunity to connect with staff about difficult issues in a positive way. There is also a parallel between this model and Key Idea 4.

The learning cycle also links into what some writers call the learning organisation.

Exercise and action planning: Training and development

Review how you manage training and development for your team.

....

....

....

....

....

....

....

How could you improve this?

....

....

....

....

....

....

....

....

Lever 4.10: The power of expectations

There has been a considerable amount of work around how a manager's expectations of staff can affect their team members' performance.

Simply put, it does seem that if a manager expects a team member to fail then there is a strong possibility that this will happen, even if the member of staff had the potential and some commitment to succeed. Similarly when a manager expects a team member to succeed, and manages to communicate that expectation, then there is a strong possibility that this will happen. These are known as a self fulfilling prophesies.

This is well known in education. Many education authorities stress how important it is for teachers and all other staff to raise their expectations of children's achievements, as well as those of the children themselves and their parents and guardians. Some academics say that, for children and education, it is not poverty that matters as much as the poverty of expectation.

This has a parallel with management. The leverage point is for managers to manage their own expectations of staff members- to behave and project a positive expectation that staff will perform well. Again, this is cheap in that it is simply part of the ways that a manager behaves on a day to day basis. This is a more sophisticated version of managers just being positive and optimistic.

Care must be taken to remain realistic, staff cannot always achieve simply because we tell them they can. However, it remains a useful lever for improving performance.

"Whether you think you're going to win or you think you're going to lose, you're probably right." Vince Lombardi

What Works 20: Working on strengths

Buckingham and Coffman's research indicated that successful managers focused almost entirely on the strengths of their staff, built on these and worked around their weaknesses by trying to find other staff to do those tasks. They said that this not only resulted in teams being successful, achieving goals, but also in powerfully motivated staff. They got to do tasks that they were excellent at and to do these very frequently.

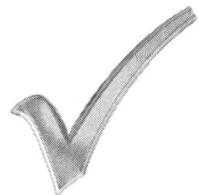

What Works 21: The power of expectations

MacGregor, an American management researcher, indicated that there are two types of managers-

> Theory X managers had a pessimistic view of their staff. They fully expected them to fail, felt that they only worked for money, were not creative and reacted negatively to a challenge and would see positive, developmental feedback as a weakness on the manager's behalf.

> Theory Y managers, on the other hand, had a positive view of people. They thought they reacted positively to challenges, wanted to develop and to do a good job for more than just their wage. Theory Y Managers thought that most people were creative and flexible.

The point here is that Theory X and Y managers had different mindsets. However, these mindsets forced their behaviour in certain ways in line with their views.

More importantly, staff in a Theory X manager's team, would begin to behave in a Theory X, negative way. Similarly Theory Y teams would begin to behave in positive, Theory Y, ways.

These managers had set up self fulfilling prophesies.

We can see from this that the way that a manager thinks, their mindset, can dramatically affect the performance of their team.

This was repeated with school children in Rosenthall and Jacobson's study, where the teachers' attitudes and expectations radically affected the children's academic and, sometimes, even social progress. In this case progress at school was more connected to the teacher's attitude to the child and their subsequent behaviours than the child's actual abilities.

Another researcher (see Livingston), bringing together a number of studies, noted that:

"If managers think that employees will perform poorly, they can't hide their expectations. Indeed, when managers think they're concealing their low expectations, they show through the most. Their high expectations often do not come through clearly enough.

Managers' beliefs about themselves influence how they view and treat their employees. Superior managers have high expectations based primarily on what they think of their own abilities to select, train and motivate people. They give up on employees reluctantly, because that means giving up on themselves."

**Exercise and action planning:
Expectations of your team**

Review your own expectations of your team, one by one. What sort of self fulfilling prophesy might you be setting up with each of them?

....

....

....

....

Can you identify a key strength for each member of your team? Document this. Do you play to this strength? Any action points here?

....

....

....

....

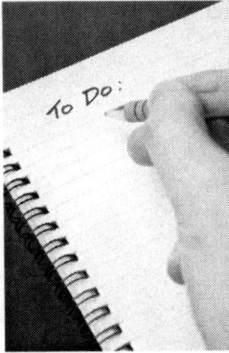

Lever 4.11: Building a Platform

Sometimes a staff member seems to have everything in place for high performance: they are committed and motivated; have a good set of skills and knowledge; the right amount of work; are capable and we have a good team culture. Yet they still seem to struggle, with poor or average performance. In some cases the performance issue arises in part from their lack of self- management; they do not have a sound, robust platform to build their performance.

This platform is the boring but essential bit. It consists usually of:

➢ Good diary systems with reminders

➢ Have a strong to do list methodology that works

➢ Document and filing systems

➢ Never forget systems

➢ A tidy desk

➢ A tidy office

➢ Control over your work

➢ Good environment to work in

➢ Strong, relevant IT support

➢ Quick, effective access to information and resources

Etc...

As a manager you can help your staff with this. The platform is not good performance itself, but is a necessary condition for it.

Lever 4.12: Role Modelling

This Lever has been mentioned before, and how managers model the behaviour that they want in staff (or alternately how they unconsciously model behaviour that they do not want) features in a lot of research on performance management in organisations.

Given the other levers in this Step, this could mean, for example:

➢ As well as giving feedback, a manager should not just accept feedback from their team members but should actually, positively invite it and plan for it. For example, make feedback to the appraiser an agenda item during appraisal.

➢ The manager having clear goals, shared with the team, which they consciously and persistently pursue.

➢ As well as helping staff to train and develop, the manager should also take their own development seriously. A lot of managers persuade staff to go on courses, saying how important development is, but never involve in this themselves. This is negative role modelling.

➢ If a manager has a negative, can't do, cynical, Theory X mindset, then it is likely that their staff will catch aspects of this. Alternatively, if a manager has a realistic but positive, on the whole can do, Theory Y mindset then this can be communicated to the team.

Lever 4.13: Policies and Procedures

Managers need to use their organisation's policies and procedures properly for three main reasons:

➢ They are usually designed to positively help you do your job properly.

➢ They will make sure that what you do is legally defensible

➢ They provide a protection to staff to ensure that they are being treated fairly and legally.

Lever 4.14: Discipline and Dismissal

We need to remember that this will always be a possible lever for a very small number of staff, probably one that is pressed only after all of the others have been tried.

We need also to remember:

➢ When using all of the levers we need to document what we have done and the lack of progress.

➢ To take careful account of the relevant company policies.

➢ Always, at the earliest opportunity, consult with your human resources department or, if you are in a small company a good employment lawyer.

Lever 4.15: Confidence and Support

Dealing with staff performance issues can be difficult. Many managers, across a range of organisations, say that what can stop them from taking needed, decisive action is lacking confidence that their plan will work, will somehow backfire on them and that they will not get support. This can apply to dealing with both high and poor performance.

There are some ways to begin to tackle this:

➢ Continue your present good practice and build on the ideas in this book.

➢ Plan to develop yourself further in this area.

➢ Discuss these issues with colleagues, support each other.

➢ Meet with your manager to discuss performance management issues.

➢ Get to know your organisation's policies and procedures in this area.

➢ Contact your staff development unit for help or find a good external consultant/trainer.

What Works 22: Balancing inquiry and advocacy

Two American writers and consultants, Roberto and Garvin, looked at how managers engage with their staff. They were interested in:

➢ How we make the best possible decisions and do the most effective problem solving.

➢ Then how we try to make sure that the decisions we make are actually implemented.

They found that the process that a manager uses in engaging with their staff is important here, not just the actual decision that we make. Roberto and Garvin identified two ideal types of process, at each end of a continuum:

Advocacy: In this style the manager (and to an extent their team members):

➢ Go into situations with a closed mind, they are relatively reluctant to be swayed by the debate, they know the right answer.

➢ Work in situations where power is more important in decision making and problem solving than intelligence, data and communication.

➢ Is interested in their own hierarchical position as much as getting things done.

➢ Looks to always defend their own position.

➢ When involved in discussions with other managers, they are concerned only with their own team and their own individual interests rather than taking a "corporate view"

➢ Is relatively disinterested in diverse, creative, innovative views about performance and problem solving.

This whole approach can lead to a perception of winners and losers and there are usually issues around implementation-things do not get done.

Inquiry – in this mode the manager (and perhaps their team as well):

➤ Goes into situations with a good degree of open mindedness, "I know what I think about this person's performance level and why it is happening, but I will try to listen and be open to other accounts."

➤ Makes decisions and solves problems based on intelligence and data, rather than just power.

➤ Participates in real collaborative problem-solving

➤ Raises ideas about what is going on and what we can do about it, testing these ideas out against the data and our intelligence and experience, and then identifying flaws and positives in each idea.

➤ Thinks deeply about issues

➤ Goes for systemic, lasting problem-solving and decision making about performance issues.

➤ Presents balanced alternatives

➤ Is absolutely clear about what is negotiable and what is non-negotiable about performance issues.

➤ Accepts criticisms

➤ Cultivates, encourages minority views

➤ Works for innovation, creativity

➤ Always looks for as much collective ownership of decisions as possible, which usually means that there are fewer implementation issues and then decisions tended to get acted on.

Garvin and Roberto found that:

When managers positioned themselves towards advocacy:
- The decisions and problem solutions tended to be of less good quality
- There was more resistance toward the decision around the performance issue
- Usually slower or even non-existent implementation, at best an apathetic attitude because the staff member could think, "Well this just might be the best thing to do, but I really don't like the way we went about it, the process, so I'm not going to push this action plan, in fact I might just push against it."

When managers tended to use the inquiry style then:
- They and the team member tended to make better decisions and problem solving around issues
- There tended to be less resistance to the decisions by individual team members
- Therefore more of the decisions were implemented, even by reluctant staff because they tended to feel that, "Well I still don't particularly like what I need to do to address this performance issue, but at least the process we went through seemed good, thorough and fair, so I'll give it a go."

The implications for managers doing performance management are that they should, as much as possible, move away from advocacy and towards inquiry:
- It means that the collective decision they make about a performance issue is more likely to a good one.
- They have a better chance that the person involved will try to implement that decision
- The manager will have less chasing up to do
- The team can perform better overall

Though we need to remember that this is not the same as "democracy", which probably would not work in dealing with some reluctant poor performers. As managers we still have some aspects that are non-negotiable. For example: "Whatever happens, your performance must improve to an acceptable standard, that is not up for grabs."

Lever 4.16: Inquiry

Based on What Works 22, balancing inquiry and advocacy, managers should search for ways to bring an inquiry approach as much as they can into their performance management. They should use the process to solve performance issues in the best possible way, to get ownership from staff of decisions and to get the best chance of implementation.

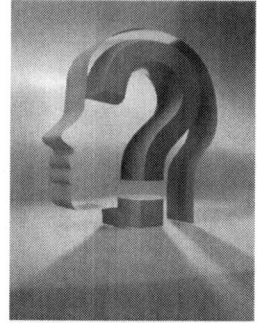

Exercise and action planning: Inquiry

Identify specific ways in which you can experiment with using inquiry in your performance management at work, list these.

....

....

....

....

....

....

....

....

....

....

Have a go at implementing your ideas.
How effective were you?

....

....

....

....

Lever 4.17: FCSC

This is another rough and ready idea that managers can use to help staff with their performance. It has added value in that the team member can use it in their everyday work.

FCSC stands for:

- ➢ Focus
- ➢ Control
- ➢ Sense of Urgency
- ➢ Clarity

These factors overlap, and once again can give a manager and their team a better grip on short and long term performance.

➢ **Focus**
The manager works with the staff member to make sure that they are doing the right things most of the time.

In their everyday performance, almost on a minute by minute basis, does the team member do things that support their explicit goals? Are these goals consistent with team goals and organisational purpose? Are they distracted by the hurly burly of organisational life, by other people's demands of them, by lack of concentration?
For example, for a fee earning lawyer, exactly how much non-chargeable time do they spend every week compared to chargeable time.

➢ **Control**
How much does the team member control their performance and activities and how much are they controlled by other people, events and crises?

In their everyday work performance, how much do they plan ahead, do they stay calm and collected when unexpected things happen that threaten their performance achievement? In team projects, do colleague have confidence in this person?

➢ **Sense of Urgency**

Does the staff member pursue their projects with dash and pace?

Does this team member invariably achieve deadlines on work, particularly those projects with ferocious time constraints? When involved in projects with colleagues, do they infect them with a strong sense of urgency, motivating them to work fast and always keeping a wary eye on deadlines?

➢ **Clarity**

Is the team member clear in all their dealings around performance?

When involved in team projects does this staff member give clear instructions, does everyone involved know exactly what is required of them? Are they clear in their engagements with customers and colleagues? Do they come to meetings with you well prepared and do they follow agreed actions? Do they use a variety of clear ways to communicate their instructions and ideas with interested parties? Can they clarify new ideas they have to improve performance and implement innovations?

Conclusion

This 4 step model, supported by the 5 Key Ideas, is designed to help you manage the performance of your staff in a practical, rough and ready, fair, positive and effective way. It is meant to clarify what can be a difficult area. It will help lead to continuously improving performance by your individual staff and the team as a whole.

Chapter 4:
Action Planning -
Putting it all Together

"An idea not coupled with action will never get any bigger than the brain cell it occupied." Arnold Glasow

Chapter 4:
Action Planning -
Putting it all Together

This is quite simple.......

✓ Scan again through all of the exercise and action planning sections and the levers in this book.

✓ Prioritise - identify which actions you are committed to, which you want to pursue. Document these.

✓ Identify some quick wins, actions you can try over the next week or so and list these.

Yes I know this is not easy. However, my work with managers over many years convinces me that improving your skills at performance management will make you an even better manager. It will help to grow your team collectively and individually and help you build a successful business.

The way ahead - some more ideas:

➢ Firstly keep your action plan going and keep experimenting.

➢ Carry this book with you and set some dates in your diary to review progress and set new goals for your performance management.

➢ Get together with your manager, mentor, coach or other managers to really discuss these issues. You may find that other managers are struggling with some of the same issues as you. Together you can get better answers to knotty problems.

➢ To start off, go through the scenarios on the next few pages and really have a go at working out what you would honestly do to tackle them. Then look at my suggestions and see what you think and re-read the relevant parts of the book.

Real Life Issues and Options

You've covered many ideas for performance management in the 5 key ideas and the 4 steps with their levers. Now it's time to integrate that knowledge with some scenarios. The idea of these short scenarios is to get you thinking about how to apply the ideas from the book to real life performance management in your own work. Remember apply them to your own environment and if possible even have a person in mind whilst you think about the possible solutions.

ISSUE 1: "He does just about OK, never really well, and timekeeping's a bit off at times. The problem is nothing is extreme, so it's hard to tackle."

Options to solve issue 1:

* Work out where just good enough is on the performance continuum (Key Idea 2). Is he worth his wage for instance? The timekeeping issue makes this more serious. You could lay down a firm standard on this, absolutely clarify your firm expectations.

* Consider Stage 1 of the model presented in Chapter 3, firstly setting clear standards and goals with this team member, then moving on to measuring his performance.

* Then you need to find out what's going on. Why is he performing like this? Go through the C7 model (Lever 3.4) with him (if you can), or just think about it yourself and draw some conclusions. If you think the major issue is commitment then you have a hard decision to make. You will need though to go through the other C6. Remember he is responsible for his own performance as well. Lever 3.5 could also give you an angle on this, QQRTPS.

* You will want to consider the impact this person's under performance is having on the other team members and on team culture (see Key Idea 5). If you do not act on this, then mediocrity and sloppy, unprofessional timekeeping could become embedded in the culture and this will track through to overall performance- see Lever 1.7.

* One approach some managers would use would be start from zero, be open with this person and make a clean start. Use Lever 1.1 and Key Idea 3, the performance management delivery system, to progress with a sense of urgency, plan for him to catch this.

* Keep on going, be persistent.

ISSUE 2: "This person is fantastic, she always does better than I expect, she uses her initiative, it's fire and forget, brilliant to work with, a real asset. Trouble is, I think she's getting a bit cynical. I can't give her more money, and she sees some of her colleagues who are nowhere near as good as she is getting rewarded, paid, exactly the same as her."

Options to solve issue 2:

★ Look for ways to keep this person fired up, motivated and interested. Give her preferential treatment when handing out juicy projects and assignments. Work with her to set stretching goals- see What Works 10 and use Lever 1.1 in a really ambitious way. Ask her what specifically motivates her at work, and then try to provide it- see Lever 4.3. Very often top performers like to get involved more in the big picture (see Levers 1.2 and 4.7). You could also use aspects of Lever 3.5, checking out that you are giving this team member lots of quality work rather than just piling on the quantity, which is sometimes the temptation with top performers.

★ Check out the performance of the other team members. If they are really below standard then this can demoralise the excellent performer. Tackle any performance deficits as soon as you can. High performers often want to see that their manager is at least trying to sort this issue (see What Works 2).

★ Work on team culture- move toward a performance culture, see Lever 1.6 and What Works 6, 7 and 8. For example, you could meet with the team to explicitly look at and document what would make a positive culture, identifying specific behaviours (eg. we always turn up on time for meetings, we always actively listen to each other) as well as just general points (eg. we respect each other). Then this team culture could be displayed and be acted on by everyone, with the manager having a crucial part to play in role modelling (see Lever 4.12)

★ Be as ingenious as you can in rewarding this person. Some sectors make this hard so you have to be creative. One straightforward was to do this would be to simply ask the person the equivalent of, "In return for your terrific performance what can I/the team/the company do for you?" or "What do you really like doing at work?" and then help them to achieve their desired outcome. In many conventional organisations this is not easy, particularly, for instance, in some parts of the public sector. When I worked in a large public sector organisation I had a superb manager who would reward high team performance by giving everyone extra holidays, despite the rigid bureaucratic rules. We were secretive about this as she was breaking the rules. However, our team consistently out-performed every other part of the organisation despite our extra holidays!

ISSUE 3:   "He is so good, willing to give everything his best shot and always delivers. I want to give him the most interesting work but the others in the team will just complain that 'it's not fair' though none of them is anywhere near as effective as this person."

Options to solve issue 3:

* ⋆ Firstly, some of the options offered for issue 2 apply here.

* ⋆ On the fairness issue, what you can try to do is to make sensible connections between performance and response rather than "stupid" ones- see Key Idea 1. The manager here needs to be tough and make hard decisions, patiently explaining to all team members that you are connecting performance to reward as best you can and that the same reward will apply to them when they raise their performance. You should also, of course support and develop them as much as you can so that they do raise their game- see Levers 4.3, 4.9, 4.15 and 4.16.

* ⋆ At the same time try to embed this person's approach in a performance culture, see Lever 1.7 and What Works 6, 7 and 8.

* ⋆ A key point for the manager here is do they make the easy decision and treat/reward everyone equally despite different individual performances. The underperfomers will be happy with this and your high performers will be aggrieved. Alternatively, you could make the hard decision to reward high performance. The top performers will be happy but the poorer performers may not be. Your role as a good performance manager would be to tackle this conflict. If you have gone through Step 2, measuring staff performance of the 4 step model in chapter 3 then you will have some good data to use in these difficult but necessary discussions with some team members. Good performance management is not easy.

ISSUE 4: "We don't really produce anything here that is concrete, measurable, we just support - do the admin. Even though I'm pretty sure I know who's pulling their weight and who's not, I can't prove it, so I don't feel I can do anything."

Options to solve issue 4:

* This can be a tough one for managers but some headway can be made through hard thinking, creativity and working with staff on this issue.

* We could try for some form of informal and systematic feedback from the people we supply a service to, for example number crunching, see Lever 2.1. We could possibly push this, where relevant, to proper service level agreements. Alternatively as a manager you could wander around getting impressions from service users in an informal way.

* Work with each member of staff using the QQRTPS (Lever 3.5) model in a very collaborative way, admitting that some of the six strands may not always be useful for everyone, all of the time in every role- see Lever 3.5. The manager could ask each staff member to prepare for the meeting by documenting what they see as the QQRTPS for their role. Such positive engagements with staff could also have a positive Hawthorne effect (see What Works 4) on their performance.

* Simultaneously we could use a version of Lever 1.1, roles and goals, with each staff member.

* At the same time trying to get them to self-monitor and adjust their own performance as they go (Lever 2.6).

* As well as this the process that the manager uses in engaging with staff could be important, adopting a subtle inquiry rather than an advocacy approach- see What Works 22 and Lever 4.16.

ISSUE 5:   "What seems to happen here is any time I try to tackle poor performance, I'm seen as bullying the member of staff. So we just seem to do nothing and let everyone just carry on and this is really unfair to the good workers."

Options to solve issue 5:

⋆ This is another tough issue. Firstly a good, honest and early discussion with your human resources department would be helpful here (Lever 2.7). What is usually crucial in situations like this is that you get the clear support of your own manager, especially if it looks as though there is going to be some serious repercussions at the end of the day. If you are a small company and do not have a dedicated HR department then build a good relationship with a friendly employment lawyer.

⋆ Make sure that you get as much hard data as you can about staff members' performance (see Step 2, Chapter 3) and work with staff on setting SMART goals for their role (see Stage 1, Chapter 3 and Lever 1.1). The manager needs to be as objective as they can at all times, see Levers 2.1, 2.9 and 2.8. Additionally the QQRTPS model (Lever 3.5) could possibly help.

⋆ Check out that you are using good process here in engaging with staff, trying as much as you can to go with inquiry rather than advocacy, see What Works 22 and Lever 4.16. The manager might also want to work on their own emotional intelligence and leadership, so that they can have the best possible impact on team members as well as staying resilient during tough times (What Works 15 and Lever 4.2).

⋆ Check out any poor performance against the C7 model (Lever 3.4). Are you sure that the reason has nothing to do with capacity, you are allocating that person simply too much work? With confidence, is your engagement with staff oppressive in any way? You might want to get some feedback on your own leadership styles- see Levers 4.2 and 4.5 and What Works 18 and 19.

⋆ Finally are you a Theory X or Theory Y manager? Have you considered the power of expectations and the possible impact of self fulfilling prophecies? See What Works 21 and Lever 4.10.

ISSUE 6: "Our appraisal scheme is so convoluted and long it's just a struggle to get the paperwork done- I see that my only goal is completing the forms for all my staff and then filing the stuff away. I don't think it makes much actual difference to the company, except waste time. We are not even allowed to look at performance, it's just about personal development."

Options to solve issue 6:

* This is another difficult issue, and sadly common. The glib response is scrap your system and start again- build one that works. Remember that any delivery system needs to be a profit and not a cost centre, to give more back than you put into it, see Key Idea 3 and Lever 3.1. Go back to the business' strategy, what is it trying to achieve and does this appraisal scheme help in any way (Levers 1.2 and 4.7).

* Going with the above means the manager has a difficult job of facing upward in their company to try to get organisational change, trying to use influence and inquiry instead of conventional power (What Works 22 and Lever 4.16).

* Alternatively, you could become a rebel. If you cannot change the organisation globally then make performance management effective locally in your team. Amend the company scheme to make it work better and, specifically, to look at more than development, which is just one goal of appraisal (see Key Idea 3). After all, managing performance is surely a key aspect of the manager's role and, indeed, a legitimate one.

ISSUE 7: "I've just inherited a team. Everyone is really good, except one person. She's been in the same job for years, and from what I hear and have seen so far, she hardly does any work and never has for as long as anyone can remember. Trouble is no one seems to have even tried to tackle this. Her previous managers seem to have gone for a quiet life. I find it hard to see how I can sort this out- she'll just say "Nobody has said anything before about my work." Of course she's right- am I going to end up letting her go on with this situation?"

Options to solve issue 7:

* Firstly, probably everyone would theoretically agree that you have to sort this issue out, however difficult it may be. The old rule of thumb applies, never do nothing in the face of sub-standard performance. To prompt this, just work out how much this staff member is actually costing the business her salary plus all the add on costs!

* We probably have to discount this person's past performance, we really have no data for this. So we start from zero by establishing explicit standards, role description and goals for this team member, and it would probably be useful to do this for every member of the team as well, Chapter 3, Stage 1 and Lever 1.1 are useful here. We could also use the practical C7 and QQRTPS models to reinforce our explicit expectations here (see Levers 3.5 and 3.4), always remembering to confirm everything on paper (Lever 2.8). Continually clarify your expectations of performance in as positive way as possible- try to set up a self fulfilling prophecy of success rather than failure- see Lever 4.10.

* This is going to be a tough time. As a manager you will need your emotional intelligence and resilience to get through this successfully (Lever 4.2 and What Works 15) as well as the support of your manager and the HR department (see Lever 2.7).

* A key aspect of your plan for tackling this performance issue will be to measure this person's, and indeed everyone else's, performance accurately over the next few months in particular. All of the material in Chapter 3, Stage 2 will be relevant here, as well as Levers 1.3, 4.1 and 4.4 and Key Idea 3 in Chapter 2.

* As usual, be aware of the cultural impact that this person's performance can have on the other top performers, and keep working on a high performance team culture, see What Works 6, 7 and 8, Key Idea 5 in Chapter 2 and Lever 1.7.

ISSUE 8: "I manage one person who works really hard- he's always rushing around, always busy. But there's a problem. I'm not sure how effective he is. I have doubts that he's doing the right things, that he's just busy. Because, he works so hard it seems mean to have a go at him."

Options to solve issue 8:

* It is mean to have a go at him. However, there is possibly an important performance issue to be tackled here that will benefit both the business and perhaps this team member. He may be mistaking activity for progress and need to get real help from you to sort this. Firstly, we can start to set this person's day to day behaviour in a strategic context (see Levers 1.2 and 4.7). Does he contribute to the business' goals, or by not focussing does he actually waste time even though he is working hard? We could work with this person and try out a few things.

* Explicitly clarify roles and goals (Levers 1.1 and 4.6 and Chapter 3, Stage 1) and then track whether what this person actually does helps him to achieve his objectives. If possible get them to do self-tracking (see What Works 13). Try to work out if the team member is paying unhelpful attention to distractions rather than the core of his role and if the reason for this is hang-ups rather than set-backs (see What Works 9).

* Try out the QQRTPS model with this staff member, Lever 3.5. Specifically pay attention to the scope, is he doing his job or someone else's and is he therefore spending resources on tasks that he should not be doing?

* The FCSC model might be useful to understand what is going on and plan action (see Lever 4.17).

   So we would work on:

➤ Focus - is this person spending his time doing the right things?
➤ Control - is he rushing about because he is not in control of his workload responsibilities?
➤ Sense of urgency - he certainly seems to be moving about with speed, but is this misdirected?
➤ Clarity - is he absolutely clear about what he needs to achieve and the scope of his role?

ISSUE 9: "I try to tackle poor performance, to do the best thing even though it's hard, but my manager just won't support me. He seems to just advise us to wait and see if things fix themselves. They never do, they just get worse. I think he just wants a quiet life, but I'm not sure what I can achieve without his support."

Options to solve issue 9:

* The honest response to this issue is without your manager's support you probably cannot achieve anything with poor performance in your staff, particularly if this performance is seriously sub-standard. However, before giving up and then either living with the situation or moving to another job, there are a couple of things that you might try out.

* Gather hard and soft data on the poor performance and how it affects the bottom line for the team and the business (see Chapter 3 Steps 1 and 2 and Chapter 2 Key Idea 1) and present them to your manager.

* At the same time you might want to try to performance manage upwards by trying to influence him and change his management behaviour, perhaps by using clever, persuasive inquiry- see Lever 4.16 and What Works 22.

* You could by-pass your manager and go straight to the human resources department, see Lever 2.7. In some circumstances you might even want to go to the top person in your organisation to let them know your issues!

* If you can solve the support problem, then the advice on tackling poor performance from the other scenarios could be relevant.

ISSUE 10: "He's two years from retirement, he just turns up for the social life, chatting and distracting the others. Everyone says just leave him to it. It's too much bother for just two years. I can understand this, but why should he get good pay for doing nothing?"

Options to solve issue 10:

* This, sadly, is another fairly common lament. This always leads me to what seems to be a rule of life in performance management. This is that the easy management decision (in this case leave him to it, do nothing) is almost always the wrong decision and the hard management decision (do something about this) is almost always the right thing to do.

* To help us decide we can count the financial cost of doing nothing, that is this person's annual salary x two. Actually it is worse than that if you factor in the cost in him distracting others' work performance and the on-costs of employing this person-some organisations estimate that the cost of employing someone is between two and two and a half times their salary.

* We can count the cultural cost of employing this person. The impact he has on team and individual morale (see What Works 8 and Lever 1.7).

* We might also look at the possible cost if this person or his role has a direct impact on the service that we give to customers and clients.

* At the end of this calculation the manager can still decide to do nothing.

* Alternatively you can commit to action, doing something. Remember very often, one of the things that top performers want from their manager, that keeps them committed to their own high standards, is that the manager tries to tackle poor performance in the team, see Chapter 2 Key Idea 2 and What Works 2.

* We could use the C7 model to tackle this issue (see Levers 3.4 and 3.2). Remember that if the reason for poor performance is commitment then the manager has more hard decisions to make.

* There are other actions you could take, pretty much every Lever from 4.1 to 4.17 could be relevant here.

* Finally, make sure you get the support of your own manager and the HR department in trying to solve this issue (Lever 2.7).

ISSUE 11: "The atmosphere in the team is poisonous, and she's the main cause of it. But it's difficult to do anything about it, she seems to do her job OK and when I have tried to talk about her attitude she says this has nothing to do with what she's paid for and none of my business, that she's not paid for her attitude, but just for turning up. What can I do?"

Options to solve issue 11:

⋆ This is another fairly common situation, nothing that concrete that a manager can put their finger on, but picking up that the climate in the team is not good, people are not comfortable, happy. This team member is right in saying that she is not paid for her attitude. She is wrong though in saying that she is paid for just turning up. She is paid to behave in certain ways, to perform and achieve goals. Further, there does seem to be a real connection between team culture and performance (specifically see What Works 8). So if she is behaving in ways that possibly impact negatively on culture, this will reduce performance levels and is therefore your business to sort out - see Chapter 2 Key Idea 1.

What can this manager do?

⋆ Firstly you can work at identifying the specific behaviours and goals that you want from this staff member (Chapter 3 Stage 1, Levers 4.6 and 1.1). Make those clear to her, record them (see Lever 2.8) and then, with her, monitor them. Throughout this the manager can provide effective feedback to the team member (see What Works 18 and 19, Lever 4.5). The key element here will probably be the resilience and persistence of the manager, and your emotional intelligence in dealing with this tricky issue, see Lever 4.2 and What Works 15.

⋆ You could also work with the whole team on identifying a positive culture, made up of specific behaviours (see What Works 6, 7 and 8). This culture or climate should be good for improving performance and good for the health and commitment of team members. Many teams do this exercise, and for most it is rewarding and effective.

⋆ Throughout this make clear your positive expectations of this team member and at the same time manage her to push these and give relevant feedback, see What Works 21 and Lever 4.10.

⋆ You might also want to experiment with using inquiry as much as you can, both with the whole team and with particular staff members, see What Works 22 and Lever 4.16.

⋆ Finally have a good plan before you start trying to solve this issue- see it as a well organised, timed focussed project, see Levers 4.1 and 2.8.

Final words

Please do remember that the scenarios have no right answers, they are just to help you apply your learning. I wish you all the best with your work in improving your performance management. If you'd like to discuss any of these issues and ideas, would like further advice or if you think I could help you or your organisation to positively tackle performance management please contact me at Steve@UoLearn.com.

Thank you

Steve Walker

Index

Further Reading

Allen, David, Getting Things Done, ISBN 978-0749922641

Becker, B; Huselid, M and Ulrich, D, The HR Scorecard, ISBN 978-1578511365

Boutall, T, The good managers' guide ISBN 978-1897587805

Britt, T, W, Black Hawk down at work in Harvard business review, January 2003

Buckingham, M and Coffman, C, First Break All the Rules, ISBN: 978-1416502661

Cook, Sarah, Creating a high performance culture through effective feedback in Training Journal, August 2001

Drucker, P, The practice of management, ISBN 978-0750685047

Goleman, D, Emotional Intelligence, ISBN 978-0747528302

Boyatzis, R; McKee, A and Goleman, D, The New Leaders, ISBN 978-0751533811

Goleman, D, Leadership that gets results in Harvard Business review, March-April 2000

Handy, C, Understanding Organisations, ISBN 978-0140156034

Hay Group, Engage employees and boost performance, 2002

Hertzberg, F, One More Time; How do you motivate employees? in Harvard Business Review, January 2003

Davies, J, K, Higher Education Staff Development Agency-, Managing to effect in Higher Education- February 2002- Briefing Paper 96

Kandola, R and Fullerton, J, Managing the Mosaic- Diversity in Action, ISBN 978-0852927427

Kaplan, R and Norton D, The Balanced Scorecard- Translating Strategy into Action, ISBN 978-0875846514

Laughlin, C, Feedback in Training Journal, April 2000

Livingston, J, L, Pygmalion in Management in Harvard Business, January 2003

Love, C, Managing Performance in Training Journal, August 2000

Management Charter Initiative, www.management-standards.org

McCarty, P, A, Effects of feedback on the self-confidence of men and women in Academy of Management Journal 29 (1986)

McGregor, D, The professional manager, ISBN 978-0070450936

Nicholson, N, How to motivate your problem people in Harvard Business Review, January 2003

Newman, Martyn, Emotional Capitalists, ISBN 978-0470694213

Pietersen, Willie, Reinventing Strategy, ISBN 978-0471061908

Pirsig, Robert, Zen and the Art of Motorcycle Maintenance, ISBN 978-0099322610

Ramsden, P, Learning to Lead in Higher Education, ISBN 978-0415152006

Roberto, M. & Garvin, D, What you don't know about making decisions, Harvard Business review Sept 2001

Rosenthal, R and Jacobson, L, Pygmalion in the classroom, ISBN 978-1904424062

Senge, P, The Fifth Discipline, ISBN 978-1905211203

Terpstra, D,E; Olson, P,D; Lockman, B, The effects of Management By Objectives on Levels of Performance and Satisfaction among University Faculty in Group and Organizational Studies, September 1982, pp 356-366

Thatcher, J, Motivating People via feedback in Training and Development, July 1999

Notes:

Universe of Learning Books

"The purpose of learning is growth, and our minds, unlike our bodies, can continue growing as we continue to live." Mortimer Adler

About the publishers

Universe of Learning Limited is a small publisher based in the UK with production in England, Australia and America. Our authors are all experienced trainers or teachers who have taught their skills for many years. We are actively seeking qualified authors and if you visit the authors section on www.UoLearn.com you can find out how to apply.

If you are interested in any of our current authors (including Steve Walker) coming to speak at your event please do visit their own websites (to contact Steve please email Steve@UoLearn.com) or email them through the author section of the UoLearn site.

If you would like to purchase larger numbers of books then please do contact us (sales@UoLearn.com). We give discounts from 5 books upwards. For larger volumes we can also quote for changes to the cover to accommodate your company logo and to the interior to brand it for your company.

All our books are written by teachers, trainers or people well experienced in their roles and our goal is to help people develop their skills with a well structured range of exercises.

If you have any feedback about this book or other topics that you'd like to see us cover please do contact us at support@UoLearn.com.

Keep Learning!

Speed Writing

Speedwriting for faster note taking and dictation

ISBN 978-1-84937-075-2, from www.UoLearn.com
Easy exercises to learn faster writing in just 6 hours.

- ✓ "I will use this system all the time."
- ✓ "Your system is so easy to learn and use."

Developing Your Influencing Skills

ISBN: 978-1-84937-004-2, from www.UoLearn.com

- ✓ Decide what your influencing goals are
- ✓ Find ways to increase your credibility rating
- ✓ Develop stronger and more trusting relationships
- ✓ Inspire others to follow your lead

Become a more influential communicator

Coaching Skills Training Course

Business and life coaching techniques for improving performance

ISBN: 978-1-84937-019-6, from www.UoLearn.com

- ✓ An easy to follow 5 step model
- ✓ Learn to both self-coach and coach others
- ✓ Over 25 ready to use ideas
- ✓ Goal setting tools to help achieve ambitions

A toolbox of ideas to help you become a great coach

Successful Business Writing

How to write excellent and persuasive communications

ISBN 978-1-84937-071-4, from www.uolearn.com

- ✓ Think about the purpose of the communication
- ✓ Create successful text for emails, letters, minutes, reports, brochures, websites, and social media
- ✓ Write effective communications to persuade people

203

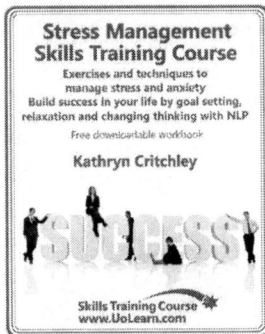

Stress Management

Exercises and techniques to manage stress

ISBN: 978-1-84937-002-8, from www.UoLearn.com

✓ Become proactive in managing your stress
✓ How to become more positive about your life
✓ An easy 4 step model to lasting change

Successful Minute Taking

How to prepare, write and organise agendas and minutes of meetings

ISBN 978-1-84937-040-0, from www.UoLearn.com

✓ Becoming more confident in your role
✓ A checklist of what to do
✓ Help with layout and writing skills
✓ Learn what to include in minutes
✓ How to work well with your chairperson

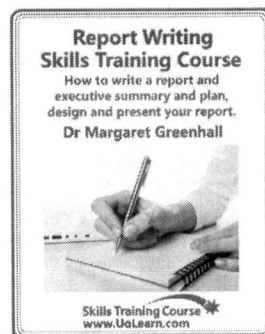

Report Writing

An easy format for writing business reports

ISBN 978-1-84937-036-3, from www.UoLearn.com

✓ How to set objectives using 8 simple questions
✓ Easy to follow flow chart
✓ How to write an executive summary
✓ How to layout and structure the report
✓ Help people remember what they read

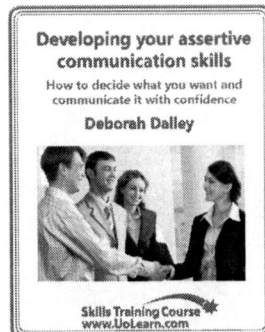

Developing your assertive communication skills

ISBN: 978-1-84937-057-8, Order at www.uolearn.com

✓ Decide what you want and communicate it effectively
✓ Develop your confidence
✓ Step by step instructions and worked examples to achieve the results you need

Lightning Source UK Ltd.
Milton Keynes UK
UKOW02f1254180214

226671UK00001B/89/P